DREEMZ

By the same author

ON THE BRINK,
with Herbert Stein

DREEMZ

Benjamin Stein

HARPER & ROW, PUBLISHERS
New York, Hagerstown,
San Francisco, London

FIRST EDITION

Designed by Gloria Adelson

Library of Congress Cataloging in Publication Data

Stein, Benjamin, 1944–
  Dreemz.
  1. Stein, Benjamin, 1944–   —Diaries.
  2. Authors, American—20th century—Biography.
  I. Title.
PS3569.T36Z466   818'.5'403   77–15900
ISBN 0–06–014071–2

---

78 79 80 81 10 9 8 7 6 5 4 3 2 1

For Al and Sally,
for John and Joan

DREEMZ

June 30, 1976

This morning I arrived at my goal—L.A. I left behind my work as a lawyer, my work as a White House speechwriter, my work as an editorial page writer for the *Wall Street Journal*, to seek gold in L.A. Palm trees instead of subways is the general idea.

I got off the plane and waited for my luggage. It was wonderful—warm, dry weather with a gentle breeze. The baggage area is partly open-air, like in the Caribbean. Near the door to the parking lot are a few beautiful girls in short shorts and tight T-shirts. This is what I came here for. Then I noticed that the girls were wearing T-shirts that were not only tight, but said something. They said: I'M BENJY'S. Behind them was Al, my contact from the studio, my friend, my benefactor. The girls ran up and hugged me while a studio photographer took pictures and other passengers looked on. This is what I have come to California for.

Outside was a studio limousine. The girls and I rode up to my hotel in the back of the limousine, and they told me their stories. All of them wanted to be actresses. The prettiest one was from a town far out in the suburbs, called Chatsworth. She had a lovely blond face with angelic blond curls. Later that night, Al told me that her manager was on parole for a weapons violation. "A real gorilla," he said. I have not come to L.A. for real gorillas, but you have to take everything together. That's only fair. I told Al how pleased I was with the girls and the limousine. "This is L.A.," he said.

July 2, 1976

From the window of my room at the Sunset Marquis I can see an apartment in which there are three girls, all in their twenties. They watch TV, eat, talk on the telephone, smoke dope. I have not seen them do anything worth mentioning. I type all afternoon at a flimsy card table covered with a beige plastic imitation-straw mat. Then, when my neck hurts from typing, I stand on the balcony and look out. Around 5 P.M., the girls come home. They wave at me and shout across the twenty yards of distance.

This evening, they shouted at me and then my telephone rang. It was the girls. They had figured out my room number at the Sunset Marquis, and then called me. I asked them to come over. They were perfectly ordinary girls. All of them were secretaries at the Bank of America. They had a clean look, with slightly larger features, all of them, than would have made them pretty. But they were friendly. They sat around in jeans and T-shirts and asked me what I did. I told them about working at the White House and the *Wall Street Journal* and coming to L.A. to write for TV. One of them, Janie, looked doubtful.

"Are you putting us on?" she asked, and then giggled. I told them I wasn't.

"Jesus," she said, "what're you doing in this dump? Why aren't you in Bel Air?"

It's a good question, and I have to think about it. Why aren't I in Bel Air? Put otherwise, if I'm so smart, why ain't I rich?

I do not want to spend too much time thinking about it, though. I have to write. I did not come here to sell shoes, but to write.

As I made my dinner tonight, though, I thought about those girls. In New York, if a man had waved at girls in an apartment, the girls would have called the police.

July 5, 1976

With the guidance of a kindly real estate woman, I found an apartment that would take both me and my dog, Mary. The apartment is perfect. It is just off Sunset Strip, and looks out over the city. The building is what my friends back in the East would call "tacky" which means that it has a heated pool, a Jacuzzi, air conditioning, underground parking, polite, helpful managers, and is almost brand new, and there is no peeling paint, no leaking pipes, no graffiti on the front, and generally none of the frustrations that give a building character.

There are all kinds of good people living here. There are hustling men in Porsches and thin leather jackets, angry-looking women in jogging suits, old people speaking with New York accents, and generally the kinds of people who are looking for life on the Strip.

My favorite tenants are the girls who bathe topless by the pool. I saw them when the manager took me around the very first time. I didn't notice it at first. I must be losing my mind. Then I noticed it and stared. The manager, a wholesome fellow, clucked disapprovingly.

"What do you think of that?" he said.

"I'll take the apartment," I said.

July 7, 1976

I have been going around to the Broadway and the May Company buying dishes and linens. I usually try to buy whatever is cheapest but does not look too horrible. Thank God, I can afford the other, more expensive stuff, but this is part of my new life. No French kitchen utensils from Bloomingdale's. Instead, I just buy something cheap, and if I decide to leave, then it's there and I don't have to take it with me.

I also rent all my furniture. I had a lot of furniture in New York that I had accumulated over the years of marriage and solicitous girl friends, but I gave it all away to a Russian Jewish immigrant. In all my life, I have never seen a soul more famished for material goods than that man. I wish that the whole scene of his carrying away my furniture could have been on TV so that people would have an idea of what living in Russia does to people. When I told that man I would give him a color TV, he became so agitated with ecstasy that he started to faint.

But I rent my furniture now. It all fits in with the Hollywood I see and want to see. It all fits in with the impermanence of everything. Especially unhappiness. People make fun of me, but I don't care. I love my rented furniture.

July 10, 1977

People keep asking me how I earn my living. I tell them that I am a bum, and that I don't know how I earn my living. But in fact I do know. I write and write and write. I write for Norman Lear and I write for a publisher who is buying a novel from me, and I write for another publisher who is buying a nonfiction book about television from me.

But none of those things keeps my feet anchored anywhere very long. They leave me free to wander around the town looking at people, looking at girls on Sunset Strip, browsing late at night at the 7–11 on La Cienega and Holloway, watching the junkies come in and out for their packages of cigarettes and Twinkies, heading out to the beach in the early morning to watch the surfers get ready for the day, watching the technicians and lighting people and sound people get a stage ready for taping one of Norman's comedies, watching the writers and producers sweat blood to get a scene done that no one will care about at all thirty seconds after it is taped.

I am also free to wake up in the middle of the night and wonder why I quit a steady job and a decent career to come out here and try to make my way. I keep thinking that no one will ever hire me to write anything again, and I will have to starve to death. Why? Why did I do it? I ask myself those questions and then I answer that I did it because I had to. I did it for love. I guess those are the same thing.

But it's not cool to worry. Out here, I meet people who have not worked in years, and they're not worried, so why should I worry? In Hollywood, you are not even expected to work steadily. It will be a struggle to adjust to that, but I'm game.

July 12, 1976

Janet Smith has made a vow. She is going to make enough money to buy a seat on the New York Stock Exchange before she is twenty-one. Janet is a beautiful nineteen-year-old girl, with fine, chiseled features, light-blue eyes and sandy blond hair. She and I met when she was bathing topless at my apartment house pool and asked to borrow my *Wall Street Journal.* She looked so good that I thought I had died and gone to heaven. L.A. magic.

I saw her a few times after that time and took her to lunch at the Palm, to impress her. It didn't work, but she still thinks of me as her friend.

Janet is from Montecito. Her parents are rich. They gave her a Mercedes 450 SL when she moved to L.A. She is supposed to be trying to be a star, and in a way, maybe she is. However, she is not making the rounds of the studios or taking acting classes or putting ads in the *Hollywood Reporter.* She is hooking, at fifty dollars a shot. "It's a hundred dollars if I have to drive to the guy's house," she said.

She will not tell me why she is hooking, except that it's for the money. "None of the usual crap about rebellion," she told me. "I just want the money."

She wants enough money to buy a seat on the New York Stock Exchange. Plus, she needs enough to start her brokerage firm. "I don't want to work for someone else," she said. "That's the fool's way out."

Her apartment has two bedrooms, just like mine. One of them is kept perpetually dark. It has red flocked wallpaper and an enormous rented bed. Next to the bed is a huge digital clock. "So people get the idea that time is money," she said.

In her living room is simple rented furniture. On a

chrome-and-glass coffee table in front of a burlap couch are piles of *Genesis* and *Viva*. There is a Sanyo stereo with TEAC tape deck against the wall next to the gas-operated fireplace. KLH speakers. BIC turntable. Belt-driven. Programmable. The best money can buy.

Janet's own bedroom is like something from Nancy Drew. There is a small wooden-framed bed next to a girlish maple dresser. On the other side of the room, next to the bed, is a dressing table with a mirror above it. Around the edges of the mirror, small photos of wholesome-looking boys and girls are spaced. At the top of the mirror is a picture of a big horse, with the ocean in the background. Her bedspread has a school crest, in blue and white.

"The big problem," Janet said, "is deciding what to do with the money. I can't just put it in a savings account, because the FBI can subpoena them anytime they want." She asked me if I had any ideas, but I didn't. It was a problem I had never had.

I keep seeing Janet at the pool. The afternoons are a slow time for her. "The really busy times," she said, "are lunchtime and the evening rush hour." She shook her head. "Really," she said, and laughed a girlish laugh, the kind that you do not associate with hookers.

She never turns tricks on the street. All her clients are referred. "Some of them are really nice," she said, "and some of them are yucky."

I had lunch with her in her apartment today, after which she showed me her new refrigerator. It was a light beige Frigidaire. Inside was one bowl of grapes, one package of presliced American cheese, three bottles of Almadén wine—one red, one rosé, one white—and a peach. There was nothing in the refrigerator freezer except ice cubes.

On the door of the refrigerator was an article from a year-old newspaper: "Twelve Ways to a Happier You." The first way was: "Just for today, I will try to be happy."

8

The second way was: "Just for today, I will try to concentrate on this day only." I did not read the other ten ways.

Janet has not offered me any freebies or shown any interest in me except as a fellow reader of the *Wall Street Journal* and, she thinks, financial expert, which I am not. I suppose that is sensible.

I think I have learned a lot about L.A. from Janet. People have big dreams, and what lies between here and there is best forgotten. It's the destination that counts. It is inconceivable that when you get there, there's no there there. It makes sense to me.

But when I thought about Janet tonight, I wondered why she had shown me her refrigerator. It does not make sense. What does it have to do with the brokerage or the hooking? It was an empty refrigerator and no more. Many people have them.

July 13, 1976

Lessons in L.A. life. My studio is considering doing a book about *Mary Hartman, Mary Hartman*. There will be a lot of money at stake. I want to do it. I talked to Al about it. In a hesitant way, I told him that maybe I could do it.

"Ben," he said, pounding his fist lightly on his Louis XIV desk, "go in there and tell Norman that you are the only person who can do it right. That's how you get things. By asking for them."

I did it, and I got the job. Now I am going to look for a Mercedes.

July 18, 1976

How important is a car in L.A.? Last night I went out with Denise W., a Jewish princess of the first degree. She pulled up in her new Austin-Healy Sprite, a low-grade sports car with a boxy, triangular look. At dinner she was snooty and condescending. Who was I? A writer, one of millions. She was the apple of her parents' eye, at twenty-nine. After dinner she graciously came back to my apartment but was standoffish. No touchie, no feelie.

After a drink, she went down to her car. It would not start. She became slightly hysterical. The auto club truck came. It still would not start. The truck did not have the right kind of hoist to tow it. She came back into the apartment dazed, humbled, a trembling shell of herself. "Take me to bed," she said in stilted but heartfelt English.

And yet I shined it on. I might have been willing to stand in for a Jaguar that would not start, but not for a Sprite. Really.

July 20, 1976

I like to shop for groceries at the Mayfair on Santa Monica Boulevard. It stays open all night, and I like to go there after 1 A.M. You can see an entirely different stratum of society from what exists on other parts of the planet. For some reason, every person who arrives at that hour, no matter of what sexual persuasion, age or race, pulls up in a used Cadillac convertible. Why? If I knew the answer, it probably would not fascinate me anymore.

The shoppers stand in front of the soft-drink section for ten minutes at a time, studying the claims of the various brands. The meat section is deserted. There is no fresh vegetable or fruit section. That's all right by me. I don't like them either.

Last night, as I stood in the checkout line and thumbed through a magazine which promised to tell me about both Farrah's and Jackie's unusual sexual appetites, I saw a familiar face.

Standing ahead of me in line, with her eyes fixed on a pile of fifty-pound sacks of dog food, stood a girl I once lived with in New York. She was a lovely girl with a pointy nose and blue-green eyes. When I knew her in New York, she had been studying ballet. She was not good at it, and I told her she should try something else. She did not like that about me. She thought it was excessively pedestrian to find fault.

She thought there were a lot of things wrong with me and God knows there were. She did me the favor of writing down a list of what she did not like. I carry it around with me, in my head.

1. You criticize everything (every single thing I do).
2. You can do everything I do better in ⅓ the time.

3. The dog dominates the house:
   a. Salivates on the table so that it is impossible to relax while eating.
   b. Sucks your thumb.
   c. Sleeps in your bed under the covers, shedding hair, among other things.
   d. Can't go outside alone and has to be watched to the point where it is an extreme inconvenience to humans.
4. Diet is monotonous.
5. Your ex-wife calls at 2 in the morning and wakes me up.
6. EVERYTHING I SAY IS KNEE-JERK, AS ARE ALL MY TASTES AND INTERESTS—THEREFORE THEY HAVE NO VALUE EXCEPT AS OCCASIONAL "LOWBROW" COMIC RELIEF.

So there she was, suddenly, in Los Angeles, at the Mayfair on Santa Monica in West Hollywood.

I called out to her. She could not have looked more surprised to see me if I had been François Truffaut (one of her idols). We talked for a while out in the parking lot, among the rusting Cadillac convertibles.

"I'm writing a book," she said when I asked her what she was doing.

"Great," I said. "What's it about? Who's the publisher?"

She gave me a pitying look. "I'm not writing it for money," she said. "It's an expression of myself."

Still, she gave me her telephone number. She did not have a Cadillac convertible. She had a Volvo with a bumper sticker that said: STOP THE WHALE KILLERS.

As I drove back to my apartment, I tried to remember why I had stopped living with the girl with the list of grievances, the girl with the Volvo, the girl with the world's most beautiful blue-green eyes. I am a veritable maniac about eyes. I could not remember, except that it had something to do with my telling her that *Mary Hartman* was greater literature than F. Scott Fitzgerald. That plus the dog salivating on the table.

13

August 15, 1976

A visit last night from my friend Mike, whom I knew in New York when he was a flunky at a major network, and who is now looking for work as a producer here. He is a handsome fellow, half Puerto Rican, half Jewish, but since I knew him in New York, he has gotten a slightly crazed look in his eyes, an aspect of peering, bulging intensity that worries me. He wanted me to talk to Norman Lear about him. I told him I would.

"Those guys like Lear, man," he said, shaking his head, "they can make you a producer overnight and then you're all set. Those are the guys who can do it. Schmucks like you and me can't do it. All we can do is sit around and wait."

I nodded. There was a worrisome edge in his voice. "I know I could be really big," he said. "Really big." He stood up and walked around the apartment. The dog got up and followed him. "If Lear can't do anything," he said, "I'm going to fucking kill myself. I'm just going crazy here, know what I mean?"

I was happy that I did not know what he meant. I hope I never do.

August 16, 1976

I have a lot to learn about California, my friend Martha
says. Martha is a housewife who moved here more than
twenty years ago. She still misses New York City. "It's
just such a great place," she says. "All different kinds of
people, doing all kinds of things together." She pulls me
aside to speak so that her gardener cannot hear. "I want
to tell you something about L.A.," she says. "Never trust
a Mexican. They literally do not know how to tell the
truth." She pauses and looks at her Mexican gardener.
"My plan," she says, "is to kill all the Mexicans in L.A."
She glares at the back of the gardener, who is trying to
pull something out of the ground. "Then I'll get the fags."

We are standing on her lawn, in Beverly Hills. The
sky is blue and the temperature could not be more perfect.
"It's different in New York," she says. "There aren't any
Mexicans there."

August 20, 1976

En route to Ma Maison last night to meet Al, I stopped on La Cienega Boulevard to pick up a girl hitchhiker. When she got in the car, I could see that she was an authentic beauty. Lovely skin, eyes, graceful nose, long, delicate fingers with lacquered nails. She carried a bundle of strange-looking newspapers.

She and the newspapers were from the bowels of a religious sect I had never heard of. Would I care to buy a subscription? For just one month? All I had to do was chant and I would get anything I wanted. I told the hitchhiker that I did not want a subscription. She insisted. It was only five dollars a month.

I told her that I had to turn off and that I would not buy a subscription. She said, far more firmly, that if I did not buy a subscription, she would not get out of the car. That was how frightening I was to hitchhikers. I told her to come to my apartment late that night and I would buy a subscription. She carefully took down the address and I thought I was rid of her.

About midnight that night, as I was preparing to sleep, she appeared at my apartment, newspapers still in her hand. She told me that I needed the newspapers, that I needed to chant.

I could dig it.

I gave her five dollars and she asked for a drink of orange juice. How, I wondered, had Nicky become a chanter?

"Well," she said, "I won't lie. I used to be a hooker until I discovered chanting." Now, she said, she got everything just from chanting, and not, as she said, "from getting it on with some old man." We parted later that night. I will reconsider about chanting.

Maybe if I chanted the right chant I could get her into bed, and then another chant would make her leave.

August 25, 1976

This morning I was sick of writing. I called the girl with blue-green eyes, the one who resented the dog, and asked her to have lunch with me. We had a greasy but delicious meal at the Palm, and then drove all around Santa Monica and the Marina peninsula. I do not know my way at all, but she did.

There were tumble-down beach cottages next to $300,000 beachfront condos. Hippies with beards and no shoes waltzed around the narrow streets carrying surfboards. Black men roller-skated on the cement boardwalk at Venice Beach.

The girl with blue-green eyes told me that this was where "real people" lived, out at the beach, as opposed to the "plastic people" I lived with in Hollywood. This was where people who ate real food and not junk food lived, people who appreciated French movies and Jack Kerouac, not people just trying to make money "as fast as they can."

I paid for lunch, of course, and then bought her a flowerpot she happened to love. "It's from Paris, France," she told me.

She knows how I feel about "real people" and "real food" by now, so I did not say anything about it.

"Who pays for you to write and live like a real person?" I asked.

"I own part of my family's company," she said. "That's all. It's no hassle."

I told her that it might have been a hassle for some of the people in Hollywood whose families did not have companies. She looked at me like I was crazy.

"It's not a question of money," she said. "It's a question of style. Some people have it, and some people don't. That's all."

She said that just as I let her off.

August 29, 1976

Hot, hot, hot. And still it is nowhere near as hot as it would be in New York or Washington at this time. In the morning it is always fairly cool, and a breeze comes off the ocean and wafts for twenty miles into Hollywood, glides along Sunset Boulevard, up North Horn Street, and into my apartment. In the middle of the day, the sun is dazzling, but the temperature is still mild compared to the East. It is a languid, magnificent climate.

This morning I went to Universal City to see a producer who was supposed to be interested in story ideas for a new adventure show that features a crime-solving fellow with a perpetual leer. He kept me waiting for forty-five minutes in a reception room filled with secretaries who had been taken by emergency airlift from Atlantic Avenue in Brooklyn to Lankershim Boulevard in Los Angeles. As I steamed at the wait, I could not avoid noticing how similar the secretaries at Universal are to the secretaries in lower Manhattan. Why? I got up to go and wrote a message to the producer, briefly outlining the plot. At just that moment, the producer appeared and waved me into his office.

He was a beefy man wearing checked trousers made of double-knit polyester. Around his neck hung a large gold ornament that said: BE HERE NOW.

On his desk was an assortment of ashtrays from various Las Vegas hotels, plus "adult" cocktail napkins with various jokes on them. Sweat stood out on the producer's face, even though the air conditioning was working well. He put a pudgy, bejeweled finger in his nose while I told my story. After a few moments he extracted something which I did not see. My story was about intrigue and double identities in a small town, people covering up criminal pasts.

The producer listened for about five minutes and then lurched forward in his chair. He smiled a tight smile. "Mr. Stein," he said, "this is not going to be your run-of-the-mill TV cops show." He laughed harshly, as if mocking the very idea. "This will be a class presentation, sort of like, well"—and he hesitated for a moment—"sort of like Agatha Christie, but better."

He gave me a script to take home and read, then call him back. It was the script for the first episode. The killer was a renegade cop. If I had a dollar for every cops show where the killer was a renegade cop, I could buy Universal. I decided not to call the producer back. The evening breeze blows bad thoughts away.

September 1, 1976

Two weeks ago I got my Mercedes. Even before I moved here, I realized that I had to get a Mercedes. There is simply no other way unless you want to be a schmuck. In L.A., a car is everything. It is how a person relates to the world, and it is how he sees himself in the world. It's all done pretty easily. Certain cars are status cars and certain cars are not. Mercedeses are at the top of the list, but others are on it. They determine everything. Last week I went to a party jammed with Hollywood types in leather jackets, aviator glasses and plunging necklines. I am never very comfortable at parties like that. I stood in the kitchen and listened to two girls talk.

"This must really be a good party," one girl said. "There's two Rolls-Royces outside."

"Cadillac limo too," the other said.

"Definitely a good party," the first girl said.

"Really," the second girl added.

The idea that I could get a Mercedes was a long time coming. My parents thought that getting an expensive car was the height of vulgarity. When I was a child, we had nothing but Chevies and Fords. When I went to law school, well-to-do people might have an Alfa-Romeo, but display in cars was frowned on. My best friend, who was married to an authentic heiress, had a blue Dodge Dart sedan, and that was considered normal.

I was even then getting out of synch. I told the wife of the Dodge Dart that they should have got a Bentley.

"You," she said sharply, "will end up with a stucco house with a cast-iron flamingo in front."

In L.A., things are different. Al the man I respect most out here, Al, who knows everything, got a Mercedes 450

SL just before I moved to L.A. He told me I should get one too.

"The thing about getting a Mercedes," he said, "is that it shows you've *done* something, instead of *trying* to do something."

There is no doubt that while I was not earning enough to get a Mercedes I thought a lot about how I wanted one. There's also no doubt that starting about a year ago, I dreamed regularly of having a Mercedes. But still, there was an existential leap. How can a sensible person, the kind of person who went to school with people who equated stucco and flamingos with hell, spend a fortune on a car, a mere mechanical trinket? What if there was a depression? What if I lost my job? But every day, I saw those Mercedes coupes and convertibles, and I saw the people driving them, and I envied them.

For the first month I was here I rented a Plymouth Duster. It was awful. Girls would look at it and say, "I never thought this would be the kind of car you'd have." That was enough.

A former colleague from the *Wall Street Journal* told me that to get a Mercedes like that was insane. "You'll spend a thousand a year in maintenance," he said. He drove a Toyota Celica, and recommended it. I knew that if I drove a Toyota Celica, I would still dream about Mercedes coupes, and girls would still be surprised "that you have a car like that."

A Mercedes is the stuff that dreams are made of, and a Toyota isn't. Finally, after four weeks, I screwed up my courage and went to Beverly Hills Mercedes. The salesman looked at me cordially and showed a 450 SL. I frowned when he told me how much it cost.

"What's the matter?" he asked sternly. "Don't you believe in your own future?"

It was a tough question.

23

Then there was the Nazi issue. A lot of people say that Mercedeses are Nazi cars. Maybe so, but as my friend Al says, "If those Nazis in Stuttgart knew how happy their cars made this Jew, it would drive them crazy." That, for me, disposes of the issue.

Still, an existential leap was necessary over the habit of growing up and education, to spend the kind of money on a car that only *schvarzes* are supposed to spend. Yet the car beckoned, as it had since I had first seen it, low, powerful and rich-looking, reeking of success and achievement.

So two weeks ago I got my Mercedes. I bought a 450 SLC, light beige; some might say gold. I love it a lot.

The day after I got it I went on a blind date with an authentic Swedish blonde. "Is this your car?" she asked. "It's beautiful." She couldn't stop saying how wonderful it was. There was nothing she would not do when she was around the kind of person who had a car like that. Another girl who lives down the hall frequently calls me from her desk in a secretarial pool. "Why don't you come down here in your new Mercedes and pick me up?" she asks in a voice loud enough for her neighbors to hear.

I have a friend here who was a famous activist in the 1960s: Jerry Rubin. He asks me how I find girls. I shrug. John Mankiewicz tells him that I go to rock music places at closing and park my Mercedes at the curb and open the door. Girls just hop in, John says. "I wonder if Ben would let me borrow his car," Jerry Rubin asks. It's not true about the girls, but so the story goes.

I go out with a Rockefeller, a real one. "I wish I could get a car like this," she says. "I think they're just about perfect."

Now, when girls are surprised about the Mercedes,

they're surprised *up*, not *down*. That's the best thing about the car. It adds to me. It makes me feel better just to be in it. That's a superficial view, but that's life here. You are what you drive.

September 7, 1976

A visit yesterday at the studio from my friend Rhonda, whom I know from long years in New York. When I first met Rhonda she was young and pretty. That was ten years ago. She moved out to L.A. two years ago, and she looks like she has been through the mill. Her face is covered with lines and her hair is straw and unruly. She has a dour look about the corners of her mouth. She inherited some money, a small amount, and has been living on that plus her earnings as a waitress at a hillbilly restaurant in Van Nuys. She has called me a few times before, but now she is in trouble. She needs advice.

I took her to dinner at the Mandarin, an excellent Chinese place in Beverly Hills. She unraveled her story. She wanted to get married. There were about six guys she was going with steadily, by which she meant she was fucking them. That had to stop. "I can't take the pill forever," she said. "I can't just lay every guy I see anymore." So she wanted to get married.

Don, one of her gentlemen callers and a lover, wanted to marry her. He is from the "old country," which means Poland, and he is a construction worker. Rhonda's father is an investment banker and she went to Miss Porter's. That is fine with me. However, Rhonda does not know what to think about Don. "He was off women for a long time," Rhonda said. "A girl he used to go with tried to ruin his life."

"How did she do that?" I asked.

"She tried to kill him," Rhonda said, absolutely expressionless, chewing a sparerib.

"How?" I asked. "By shooting him?"

"No."

"Stabbing?"

"No."

"Poison?"

"No."

"Drowning?"

"No."

"Blunt instrument?"

"No."

"Running him over?"

"No."

"Well," I said, "I think I've covered just about everything."

Rhonda looked jubilant. "No," she said proudly, taking the sparerib from her mouth. "You didn't cover pouring Sani-Flush in his ear and then pouring in water."

I told Rhonda that I would be careful with Don. He was likely to hold a grudge against women.

Rhonda wears sequined glasses, whether as a joke or not I do not know. She took them off, put them next to her Chiao-Tzu on the plum-colored tablecloth, and heaved a deep sigh. The people at the next table, who had been discussing resorts in Mexico, turned sharply.

"I don't know," Rhonda said. "I just don't know. In a few years, no man will be interested in me at all. I'll have to become a lesbian. Then what? Maybe I'll wish I had married Don."

I had to agree that it was a serious problem. "Maybe you should move to another town and change your name," I said.

She sighed again. "I've already tried that," she said.

27

September 8, 1976

Last night I took the girl with blue-green eyes to dinner at Ma Maison. She liked it a lot. She had heard of it, she said, but she had never been there.

"I usually prefer little foreign places where a family runs the whole restaurant and serves you from their own kitchen. It's much more authentic," she said. "But this is good too." There were a lot of movie stars there, but I did not know any of them.

The girl with blue-green eyes told me that she never goes out with men, at least not much. She wondered why, looking wistful. I told her I wondered why too.

"Oh, well," she said. "Sometimes the soul must nurture itself alone."

It seemed like a funny thing to say amidst all the people talking about negative pickups and option deals and off-shore tax havens, but I did not laugh. That was why I had lived with her in New York, and that was why I loved her. Because when I had talked about why the city was going bankrupt, she had talked about 1920s architecture.

But when we got home, she would do no more than kiss me. "I'm not one of your sluts," she told me. "I don't believe in casual relationships. Getting in touch with another's soul is very important to me. I can't treat it as a joke."

She looked adorable to me, with her slightly oversize chin and her pout. "How about if I spank you for being bad?" I asked.

For an instant, her eyes twinkled, and then she said, "When men make suggestions to me like that, I tell them to take me right home."

I just grinned at her. The dog tried to grasp her wrist in her mouth.

"I don't know why you moved here," she said. "Your soul is still wandering. It has not found a home."

"Yes it has," I said. "Home is where I spank you."

She smiled for a while and then told me that perhaps my trouble was that I was spiritually thirsty. "You need to discuss things more, to analyze, to think about things."

"That's why I'm here," I said. "To not do any of those things."

After a while I took her home.

"Maybe I'll send you some things by Carlos Castaneda," she said.

"Maybe I'll break into your house and spank you," I said.

Generally I do not like to analyze too much, as I told the girl with blue-green eyes. But I know that teasing someone a lot is a sign of love. I know that.

September 9, 1976

DREAMS is taken. So is DREAMZ and also DREAM 1. But the people at the Department of Motor Vehicles said that DREEMZ was available, so that's what my license plate will be. To me, it's perfect.

September 10, 1976

Last night I drove down to Newport Beach to have dinner
with some old friends from the White House. At dinner,
we talked about politics, about the old days, about the
way Ford was blowing his opportunities. (If there's anything we old Nixon hands know about, it's blown opportunities.)

The other couple talked about the quiet routine of life
at San Clemente—the research, the long reminiscences,
the rounds of golf. My friend is now helping Nixon with
his memoirs. No one said a word about deals or who is
producing what or who has gotten rich quick or who has
left his wife. It was a quiet evening.

My friend G., an amazon of a blond Englishwoman,
smiled politely without saying anything most of the evening until the very end. We were discussing why Mrs.
Nixon smiled so much. Then G. asked a question: Do you
think Mrs. Nixon was using cocaine? G., unlike my friends
from the old days, lives in Hollywood. My friends from
San Clemente were speechless. It was a joke, I told them.

September 12, 1976

Why do I love L.A.? Tonight, just at dusk, I drove along Mulholland Drive. Bushes with white buds were in bloom. For hundreds of yards, the blossoms brushed against my car. Off in the distance I could see the mountains, shrouded with fog on the summit. In front of my car, the air was crystal clear. The sky was a magnificent deep blue, with orange and gray tints off to the west, where the sun was setting in a fiery burst. There was no traffic on the road. Ahead of me, two bluebirds ran interference, flapping their wings wildly. There were vividly colored trees everywhere by the road.

Next to me on the seat was a beautiful girl with blue-green eyes who had just touched my leg and told me that she needed to be spanked.

September 15, 1976

A sunny afternoon in a light-blue room in a Spanish-style house in the Hollywood hills. A bed next to a sliding glass door. Bamboo shades filtering out the sunlight. Out the window, the palm fronds and eucalyptus leaves flutter in a lazy breeze, making shadows on the bare walls. A bedspread of brown and white cotton in a pattern of cocoa palms. A girl with pale skin, lank hair and blue-green eyes.

I spend few afternoons like this afternoon, but each one is a diamond in my memory.

September 22, 1976

A visit from Rhonda this morning. She appeared in short shorts and a T-shirt that said: FLY ME—I'M RHONDA. She has her points, but being exactly up to the moment is not one of them.

"I need to learn how to do something," she said in her blank voice. "I want to learn how to give better head. I've been getting a lot of complaints." It seemed like a fine wish. "Can I practice on you? It's nothing personal, but we've been friends for a long time, and I know you'll be patient." I had to think about that, but only for a little while. "I like you, Ben," she said. "You know when to help a girl out."

It is hard to believe that something like that could be work, but only if you do not know Rhonda.

September 25, 1976

Before I moved here I met a beautiful girl named Sybil. She is a tall, thin brunette with lovely features and mournful brown eyes. She works as a genealogist at a small library. She also is an heiress to a substantial shipping fortune.

I took her to Ma Maison last night. She liked it, but criticized me for pretentiousness. What am I to say?

She will not sleep with me. Also, nothing below the waist. Also, nothing above the waist. Also, nothing. Normally, that would have made me fall madly in love with her, but not last night. At a certain point, I started to no longer want what I could not have. Still, I am interested in Sybil, to put it mildly. I keep seeing her lovely features and wondering when I am going to get some.

She asks me often if I only like her for her money. At first I always said no, and she would say, "I don't believe you."

Now, when she asks, "Do you like me for anything more than my money?" I tell her that I like her for her family connections more than for her money. I cannot tell if she knows it's a joke. I cannot tell if I do, either.

September 27, 1976

Rhonda came to see me again yesterday. She was afraid that she had hepatitis, but apparently she did not. "I could have," she said. "I guess I was just lucky." One of her many boyfriends had recently been rushed to the hospital with an attack.

She had an idea of how to make some money. "It's like being a baby-sitter," she said, "only I would *have* a baby." Her idea was to put an ad in the *Free Press* offering herself as a place of germination and growth of a man's seed. "The guy could come and look at me and see if I was what he wanted. If he liked me, like if he thought I had the right kind of stock, he could fuck me and I would have his baby. How much do you think I should charge?"

I told her I thought ten thousand was fair. "After all," I said, "you can work at something else while you're doing it."

"And," Rhonda added, "I could still go out and I wouldn't have to be on the pill."

"Great idea," I said.

"Do you think I could put the ad in *New West?*" she asked. "I might meet a better class of guy."

After Rhonda left, I thought about why I know so many people like her. Friends from law school, people who lead a more orderly life, have asked me about it. The basic answer, I think, is that I like these lowlife types. I greatly prefer to hear Rhonda's schemes than to talk about law or law firms. To be fair to Rhonda and her ilk, I also like to feel superior to her. That's probably not the slightest bit unusual. I also like to be with important people, the ones who talk about giant deals, or about making people President, and what television means to American culture.

There is an air of titillation, of perversity, though, about people like Rhonda. Something of the forbidden lingers around her, just as it does around Roxanne and others. If I had just wanted to lead a quiet life, I could have stayed in Washington.

September 28, 1976

Dinner last night with my friend G., a lovely English girl with an absolutely white and pale complexion and deep red lips. She has a cockney accent, far different from Laurence Olivier's. She told me in great detail about the man who is keeping her. He is an Arab who floats on a sea of oil money, towing smaller ships in his wake. His picture is often in newspaper society pages with his wife, a famous dresser in expensive clothes. "He wants me to learn Arabic," she said. "He says they're going to take over the whole world."

I did not have any advice for her on that subject. She did not think it was very important. "They'll always need hairdressers, no matter what," she said. "We're pretty much indispensable," she said, "these days."

Later that night, I got a better idea of why G. was so sure that she was indispensable. At a certain moment, G. began to wrestle with me and then turned me over. With great, sharp strokes, she spanked me several times before I realized what was going on.

"What the hell are you doing?" I asked. G. was humming to herself at a loud pitch.

She stopped her spanking suddenly as I jumped away. "Oh, I'm sorry," she said. "You just get into a habit. Do you know what I mean?"

I guess I do.

Everyone is talking about spanking, she said, and I believe her. "It really shows you care," she added. "Sometimes you can really hurt your hand." She looked sincere. "If I didn't care, why would I take that chance?"

September 29, 1976

Today is my ninety-second day in Los Angeles. I came home from looking for a house this afternoon and sat down to do some work. At about five-thirty, the telephone rang. Roxanne, a thirty-year-old woman who lives down the street from me in my apartment just above Tower Records on Sunset Strip, asked if she could come over to show me something. I told her that I was very busy.

"Oh, c'mon, Ben," she said. "It'll only take a few minutes."

"O.K., Roxanne, but let's make it very quick," I said. I figured she must want to borrow money.

A minute later, she appeared at the door in a black, filmy gownlike outfit under a thin coat. Mary, the dog, lunged at her, but I pulled Mary away.

Roxanne, a small, sandy-haired creature who looks like she was expelled from France for looking too Gallic, pushed Mary away.

"Don't let her get up on me," she said. "I don't want to ruin the surprise."

"What's the surprise?"

"Well, I can only show it to you in front of a mirror," she said.

I showed her my bathroom mirror.

"That doesn't go down far enough," she said.

I showed her another, larger mirror in my study. She stood in front of it and said, "Now watch!" as if she were going to pull a rabbit from a hat. In a slow way, she pulled up her dress to her knees, then to her thighs, then to her waist. She was wearing, under the dress, black stockings, a garter belt, and panties with a slit where you might imagine one to be.

"What is this for?" I asked her.

"It's for sex," she said, throwing her arms around me. "Doesn't this turn you on?"

"Roxanne," I said, "you're just basically sexy, but the clothes aren't what's sexy."

"Look at this," she said, and released about five ribbons, which allowed the top of her dress to come down, revealing a pink see-through brassiere over her small bosoms.

"Really great," I said. "Really."

"Well," she said, "doesn't this make you want to do it?"

"Really," I said.

"Really," pronounced "rilly," means "yes, that is so." At least south of San Luis Obispo.

Roxanne and I walked out toward the Jacuzzi. There were voices in the Jacuzzi, and when I got close, I could see that there were a man and a woman in the Jacuzzi together. They were fucking.

"The only thing that's surprising," Roxanne said, "is that it's not two men."

I went back to my apartment and took a shower. I made a mental note to remember the details of what happened.

A few minutes later, Roxanne and a gaunt woman neighbor named Muffie appeared at my apartment door. "I have a new corporate problem," Muffie said. She is trying to start a company that will clean up apartments and buy groceries and make the beds and stock liquor and unpack for young executives. Until tonight, she had planned to call it "Princess Unlimited."

"We're gonna call it 'The Compleat Swinger,' " she said. "What do you think?"

"Sounds good to me, Muffie," I said.

"Maybe you'll help me write the prospectus," Muffie said.

"I'll be glad to," I said.

40

Roxanne piped up. "Did you hear about Buffie?"

Buffie is Roxanne's former roommate, a small, angry-looking woman who moved out of our building because it was too dull. She went to live with friends in Marina del Rey who had nonstop backgammon games for money.

"What about Buffie?"

"She's in a mental hospital in Santa Monica. She committed suicide."

"What?" I asked, "She killed herself and she's in a mental hospital?" I asked. That would be something for those skeptics in New York.

"No, no," Roxanne said, giggling. "I mean she tried to kill herself."

I met Roxanne about a month ago when I was walking my dog. She asked me to come to her apartment and talk to her. She was wearing a T-shirt with nothing on underneath. Nothing on below the waist at all. This kind of thing does not happen to me very often.

Later that night she explained to me that she was a poet. She had not written anything, though. "It's all in my head," she said. "I'm just getting ready to write it down."

"Really," I said.

The next day she knocked on my door. "I want to see your bedroom," she said.

She went into the bedroom and looked carefully at the bed. "Wouldn't you like to tie me up?" she asked, throwing herself on the bed.

"I don't know," I said. "I've never tied anyone up before."

"Come on!" she said, shocked. "Never?"

"No," I said. "Never." No courses on bondage in law school.

"Well, tie me up," she said.

"I don't have any rope," I said.

"Don't you have any cord or twine?" she asked.

"No."

"Well," she said, "you must have some neckties or bathrobe sashes."

I did.

She talked a lot while she was tied up. My friend G. later told me I had done it wrong.

"You must put an apple in her mouth. Or a pear. And don't ask her what to do. Just do it."

I nodded appreciatively.

"Then you must take off your dog's collar and put it around her neck. Put on the leash, and then walk her around the apartment on her hands and knees."

"Should I keep her gagged, then?" I asked.

A disgusted look crossed G.'s face. "If you do," she asked, "how will you get her to eat out of your dog's dish?"

G. told me that I obviously did not understand the first thing about bondage. "Listen," she said. "I have a complete SS officer's uniform. If you need me," she said, "I'll put it on and come over to help."

A few days ago, Roxanne called to tell me that she was sick, had no money and was starving to death in her apartment. I told her I would buy her some groceries. She typed out a list of what she wanted at the Safeway on a piece of stationery with an engraved fleur-de-lis surrounded by roses imprinted on the bottom.

> Angel Food Cake
> Vanilla and Chocolate Ice Cream
> Cokes
> Benson and Hedges COLD

Except for tonight's adventure with the clothes, I try to avoid Roxanne. Bad karma.

October 2, 1976

I ran into some friends of my parents out here last night at the Safeway on Santa Monica in West Hollywood. Marty W. and his wife, Marian, introduced me to their daughter Marilyn. Their other children—Marvin, Marcie, Mark and Marla—are no longer living at home.

October 3, 1976

Seven or eight years ago, when I was a pitiful student at Yale Law School, I walked by a neo-Greek temple on High Street after midnight. It was the meeting place of a secret society. The name, unknown to me then, is unknown to me now. Through the windows, crosshatched with stone, came lovely melodies. The secret society was singing. In rich harmony the words "Troubadour, troubadour, sing troubadour" came floating out onto the New England air.

I imagined all of them in there, the scions of the gilded age, enjoying every moment of life, secure in the knowledge of their place in society. Golden-haired, clear of eye, lithe and thin and confident. It made me envious as I scurried past, holding my sickening lawbooks, heading back toward a dim and dismal suite. I shared that suite with a gawky fellow from Indianapolis who arose at 6 A.M. each morning to study. If there was anything that people do of their own accord more dismal than my experience at Yale, I do not know what it is. And the singing of those who were happy, just a few steps from my room, made it worse. Recently I talked to Bob Haldeman about his impending stay in the pokey compared with that time at Yale. He decided he would rather go to jail.

I think of that often when people tell me how trashy life is in L.A. I think of L.A. singing, everyone in the secret society together, singing our happiness into the balmy night air.

October 6, 1976

I have been spending a lot of afternoons with the girl with blue-green eyes. She keeps bringing me books. Huxley. Pynchon. Brautigan. "Real people."

She looks at me and tells me that living in Hollywood is ruining my soul.

"Move out to the beach," she says. "Get away from it all. Get in touch with your soul."

I think about that a lot, only because she says it so much. But the whole point of being in L.A. is to get things done, to get into the mainstream, not to get away from it all. If you want to get away from it all, you can be dead. I told that to the girl with blue-green eyes, but she did not think it was funny.

"Living east of the San Diego Freeway is a kind of death," she said, turning her face heavenward.

I think I will send that definition in to the Harvard Medical School.

October 7, 1976

This afternoon I went with a friend, a woman reporter from New York, to the Malibu Beach Colony. The Beach Colony, as it is called, is a row of about fifty houses on a beach in Malibu. Access to the Beach Colony from the Pacific is via a guarded driveway. Access from the beach is easier, across a narrow, occasionally flooded strip of sand. Access any other way is almost impossible, since the tiniest clapboard shack in the colony starts at about $400,000.

The owner of the house we visited was a middle-aged woman married to a TV producer. Her house was small and unpretentious. She bustled around, ordering the Spanish maid to give us Fresca. By the time we arrived, she had already had enough sun and was sitting inside.

Her daughter had slashed her wrists the night before and was in Santa Monica Hospital.

"It's not really as bad as it sounds," the mother said. "She does it all the time, and at least each time she goes into the hospital she loses a little weight. That's why she does it in the first place."

Far down the beach, but still in the Beach Colony, Genevieve Bujold sat on the beach playing cards, topless. She looked wonderful. "She," our hostess said, "has no problem with *her* weight."

October 8, 1976

A visit this evening from my neighbor Roxanne. She wants to make a deal with me, under the terms of which she will "satisfy [my] sexual needs" in return for my paying for her rent and her utilities. It sounds like a pretty good deal to me. Roxanne, to give her credit where it is due, has the most highly developed sexual skills I have ever encountered in many areas. I sometimes wonder if she could start a business teaching her skills to other women. They would never be lonely.

Roxanne said she would give me a sample, just to show me what a good deal it was. Just to show me what a super-fantastic deal it was, she would do it in the Jacuzzi.

That, I thought, was the pioneering spirit of bravado and salesmanship that built many great companies. Still, I had to turn down any long-term deals. Roxanne is just too unreliable. I might not be able to reach her in an emergency. I told her of my concern.

"I could get a beeper, like doctors have," she said.

October 9, 1976

Last night Sybil, my rich and glamorous friend, took me to a party of rich Gentiles at a famous decorator's studio. Sybil, who is richer than almost any person alive, was eager to go in my Mercedes, because she was afraid that people would look down at her in her BMW. She slid around the room, terrified, she said, that some rich person might make a snobby remark to her, embarrassingly grateful for my company.

Later, at my apartment, she told me why she would probably never love me. "We just come from two different worlds," she said. "You come from the world of go-getters and I come from the world of wallflowers." One of the wallflowers in her family was president of a major steel company and another is an ambassador to a western European country. I think that her resistance comes from something else entirely. She is from Boston. She told me about how she would no longer go into Bloomingdale's in New York because of the "pushy, short, buxom women in the elevator with their New York accents." I am different from those people in the elevator, Sybil says, because I am not from New York. I don't know what keeps me from punching Sybil. Probably I do know, but I do not like to admit it.

October 12, 1976

Early this morning, around 5 A.M., Mary started barking
furiously, clambering out from under the covers, racing
back and forth in the bedroom. There was a faint rapping
at my door. Gun in hand, I went to the door to listen.
More rapping, and a strained voice crying out my name.
I opened the door, and there stood Roxanne, looking
bedraggled in her nightgown. She fell into my apartment
and threw herself onto the couch.

"I'm in terrible trouble," she said. "Terrible."

"What is it?" I asked.

"I need some coke really bad," she said. "I honestly do."

"I don't have any," I said. "I hope you didn't wake me
up for that."

"Yes," she said, her voice faltering, "but you have
enough money for me to get some."

I walked right into that one. "Where can you possibly
get it at this time of day?" I asked.

"Oh," she said with surprising lightness, "there are
places."

Just at that moment, Mary started to bark furiously
again. There was more faint rapping at the door. I opened
it stealthily, and there was Susie, a beautiful, but really
beautiful, friend of Roxanne's, an acquaintance of mine,
and a junkie.

In her New England accent, Susie asked me for just
what Roxanne had asked me for.

"We really need it," Susie said. "We'll do anything to
get it."

Both of them looked at me brightly. Their nightgowns
were falling open.

"How much do you need?" I asked.

There was some negotiation and then one of life's rare and exciting occurrences. None of us was exactly gung-ho, but it was still something for the days when I live inside four walls.

As Roxanne and Susie left, Roxanne turned to me and said, "You've got to be careful, Ben. You're getting a reputation as someone who trades girls favors for sex."

I will have to think about that one.

October 19, 1976

There is a song, perhaps by Cole Porter, about Hollywood parties. In the song, the parties sound glamorous and exciting. In real life, as far as I can tell, they are different. Last night I went to a party at a rented home high in the Hollywood hills, on Sunset Plaza Drive. The house was packed with thin, angry, frustrated-looking men and women, leaning into the walls as if they were holding up the house. There was nothing left to eat or drink by the time I got there. A few people passed around miserable joints.

In a room overlooking the pool, two extremely sexy-looking girls danced with each other. I thought for a minute I would lose control of myself.

Behind me, a woman wearing a T-shirt that said I'M A VIRGIN, with large, drooping breasts and a huge Hebrew letter around her neck, was talking to a beefy-looking woman wearing a sweat shirt that said THE O'JAYS. One of the women said to the other, "So this guy calls me up and says he wants me to go down on him, give him coke and lend him my car. And the worst part is," she added, "that he showed up half an hour late."

The other one said, a little later, "I'm sick of balling these married guys. No more balling them from now on. Unless I like them."

"Really," the first girl said.

There was nothing else going on at the party, so I went home. En route down Sunset Boulevard, I stopped to pick up a girl who I thought was hitchhiking.

"I'm only going as far as Horn Street," I said.

"Fifteen dollars for fifteen minutes," she said.

"I think there's been a mistake," I said.

51

She looked hurt. She looked down at her teen-age self. "Don't you like me?" she asked.

"Of course. You're pretty." She was pretty, with curly light-brown hair and a fair complexion. But I am not yet at that stage of life, so I shined it on and went home to watch *Mary Hartman*.

October 20, 1976

"How do you think I feel?" G., my English girlfriend, asked me. "I go out with men with Ferraris and I can barely pay for my Mustang."

G. and I were having lunch at a dive in West Hollywood filled with dispirited remnants of the hippie culture. She wanted to sound me out on her plan for making some money.

"I've got a good list of men whose hair I cut," she said. "Now, if I could just find the girls to work for me, I could have a nice little operation going." G. had in mind a service with an extremely old history. "The problem is finding girls who'll do it, men who'll pay, and keeping the whole thing going."

I wondered what she wanted from me. I hoped it was not money.

It was.

"All I need is a few thousand to get it started," she said. "You can have any of the girls you want, anytime you want, plus I'll pay you back with interest."

I don't know why I keep getting these requests for money from girls. I do not like it. It may have something to do with the car, but I'm certainly not going to give up the car.

October 21, 1976

On the car radio I heard that an appliance store here is sponsoring a contest to see who can spend the most consecutive hours watching television. It is part of a promotion to sell television sets. Part of every dollar received will go to fight muscular dystrophy. It strikes me oddly that one kind of paralysis is encouraged to fight another kind of paralysis. But it's not worth thinking about.

October 26, 1976

A rock concert at the Roxy last night by a group so terrible that God, in His mercy, has obliterated their names from my memory. The whole room vibrated from their deafeningly loud, undefined music. The only thing that made it even slightly worthwhile was that there were pretty girls with lithe behinds walking back and forth by my table all evening long. Of course, that has little to do with me. I am just a miserable writer who happens to be earning a living. All around are men with thin leather jackets and gold jewelry who are rack jobbers or record producers—which means Ur-Mafia—who make fifty thousand dollars a month.

The record business in this town is unbelievable. That is where people come from nowhere and make a million dollars overnight. It is a highly fractionated industry into which money is spewing like lava. If you see someone with a Rolls convertible, he's almost always in the music business.

For a few minutes last night, I wondered if I should get into the record business. I had to shake myself out of it. There are some other goals besides money, I hope, left in my whirling brain. This morning, it all seemed like a bad dream. I am glad I got it over with quickly.

But I wonder where writers find those girls. Unless they live in my apartment house.

October 27, 1976

The girl with blue-green eyes is angry at me. She says that all I do is make fun of her, plus the dog still dominates the house, plus I have completely surrendered to the "plastic life style" of Hollywood.

"Where is your soul?" she asked. "Where is your spiritual growth coming from?"

When she asked me that this afternoon, I felt sad.

"Not everyone has a rich family," I said. "Not everyone wants to retreat. Some people want to go someplace they haven't been. I wish you'd think of that." Because I like the girl with blue-green eyes so much, she can hardly ever hurt my feelings. But this time she had.

"Why am I any more plastic on Sunset Boulevard than you are in your health food store? What the hell makes you think that anyone made of flesh and blood is plastic?"

"It's all so fake," she said.

I asked her if she ever considered that even fake somethings are also real fakes. But then I stopped that crap. Too much like law school.

"I'm not a fake," I said. "I'm not just like you, but I'm not sure which one of us is a fake."

That made her cry.

November 8, 1976

A meeting of two worlds. My rich friend Sybil and I went to an organizational meeting for a new group that will campaign for farm workers' rights. Two different slices of life put in appearances. First there were Sybil's friends, heirs and heiresses from fortunes around the country. On my left was a sandy-haired fellow with a slack jaw whose parents had had the foresight to have grandparents who owned an immense brewery. Other kids were inventive enough to have ancestors in shipping, meat packing, banking and oil. They looked slightly out of it but extremely earnest. Outside, in the enormous driveway, their gleaming BMWs stretched for a hundred yards. Each one had a bumper sticker denouncing the wastefulness of the system. BOYCOTT JAPAN, TREES HAVE RIGHTS, RECYCLE, STOP THE SEAL KILLERS.

The other faction were producers, directors and writers who were environmentally engaged. They had made their own money, occasionally forty thousand dollars a week of it, but they, too, had a social conscience. To the jeans and work shirts of the heirs, the show biz people wore tight-fitting body shirts from Hermès and hand-tailored slacks from Gucci. Around their necks hung gold jewelry. Their hair was neatly trimmed, in contrast to the shaggy looks of the heirs.

To the heiresses' "frontier woman" look of braided blond hair and baggy clothes, the show biz wives offered tight slacks from Saks and Judy's and painstakingly coiffed brown and black hair.

We sat by a pool in back of an English manor house in Bel Air. The blue of the lighted, heated pool made a lovely contrast with the white decking and the wrought-iron tables. A husband-and-wife serving couple passed among us, offering drinks and prettily laid out small sandwiches. The house was on a curving street so that I could just barely catch a glimpse of the line of Rolls-Royces on the street.

Our host, a writer who has won many awards and has houses in at least two European countries in addition to two in L.A., opened up a silver Mark Cross cigarette case and removed a custom-made Sherman cigarette. His manservant lit it with a deferential bow and a gold cigarette lighter.

Our host ran a hand through his graying locks and exhaled from his cigarette.

"I just thought I'd say," he said, with a meaningful look, "right here at the beginning, that we are all outlaws in the eyes of the Establishment."

November 10, 1976

Definition of a good time in L.A.: About three o'clock in the afternoon, Danny, a very tall former student from my academic days, called and told me that there was some "perfectly boss Hollywood nose" in town. Would I like to try it? I told him to come over and we would see.

Around 10 P.M., he arrived in patched jeans, smiling genially. Mary, the dog, leaped all over him. He fended her off and sat down, still grinning.

"This is such boss stuff," he said. I gave him a glass of orange juice and he drank it sparingly, as if it were brandy.

"You've got to try this," he said. "It's groovy."

"Really," I said.

He took from a grimy pocket a small packet of tin foil. He carefully and deliberately unwrapped it. Inside was a fine white powder, superwhite, white as snow in Vermont. There was far less than a quarter of a teaspoonful. That is, one hundred dollars' worth.

With a small silver spoon, he took a tiny amount out of the packet and placed it on the glass-topped coffee table (rented).

With a razor blade, he chopped up the already fine powder into far finer lines, about one-sixteenth of an inch wide and three inches long. He then took a twenty-dollar bill from his wallet and rolled it into a shape like a truncated straw. Grinning, he offered the straw to me. I shook my head and he said, "It's cool."

He bent his head over the coke, put the straw in his left nostril, closed his right nostril with his right index finger and sniffed up two of the lines. With his right nostril, he sniffed up the other two lines. He exhaled loudly and said, "Hotchacha," and giggled. He leaned back in the couch. I am not sure that I have ever seen anyone look that happy.

November 11, 1976

A late-night call yesterday from my rich and glamorous friend Sybil. She was lonely. Could I come over? I drove my wonderful car to Bel Air where she lives, past the mansions of long-departed movie stars, beyond their high, whitewashed walls, surrounded by slightly drooping palm trees, along curving side streets, past lookouts where the city's lights blazed for twenty miles, up to her modern house with its pool and its pictures of famous ancestors.

She sat in her expensively decorated living room looking sad. We talked for a little while. She felt worthless. How could she live in a town like L.A., where everyone was doing things? All she did was sign checks and give away money she had never earned. She once worked in genealogy, but she has given that up.

We talked more and I reassured her that she was a great girl, that everyone loved her, that she was smart. She did not want to hear it. She wanted to blow coke. I did not have any, but she did. In a few minutes, her whole mood had changed. She was more interested in me than I had ever dreamed she could be. She felt close to me. She understood me. She appreciated me. She was sorry she had made anti-Semitic comments. Just to show me how sorry, she would work as my maid for a week, free. She cried on my shoulder.

The spawn of the ghetto soothing the duchess of the gilded age.

I left with a new understanding of nothing, but with a lot of memories. That in itself may mean something, but it is probably best not to think about it. Sybil called this morning to ask when she could start working as my maid.

I think I will ask the girl with blue-green eyes if she thinks Sybil is a fake maid or a fake heiress.

I also think I'll ask Sybil to wear a little French maid's uniform with a short skirt so that I can spank her anytime I want.

November 14, 1976

Lunch yesterday with P. and my hustling friend Tony. P. is a famous, highly paid screenwriter with bad acne and a fat waistline. He is about my age and has already been nominated for two Academy Awards. Definitely a Hollywood phenomenon. We talk exclusively about girls. Every time either Tony or I mentions a girl, he looks as if his tongue will fall out.

"I can't believe it," he says. "I'm getting two hundred and fifty thousand a screenplay and I can't get laid."

I can believe it. P. can write fabulous screenplays, but there is nothing fabulous about him. Still, he should be able to do something. I think I'll send him to Janet Smith.

November 15, 1976

Recently, I had lunch with Bob Haldeman. I never met him when I was at the White House, but we have mutual friends, so we got together here. He looked friendly but slightly wary. We talked in the foyer of La Scala while we waited for a table. Then, miraculously, we were shown to one of La Scala's best tables. I had never been near it before. A waiter danced attendance on us throughout the meal. I have never had such good service. The captain stopped by to ask about our cannelloni. Bob was impressed. He thought they were doing it for me, I think. Of course, they were doing it for him. In L.A., he was still a star. He still got on TV a lot, didn't he? L.A. has a limited field of vision, but it's cool. I liked having that table.

November 17, 1976

I am trying to stay out of the cocaine trade. It is hard to turn it down, because I know that there is fast money to be made and I would like some fast money. Still, it is illegal. And still, it is extremely dangerous. Money is no good when you're dead.

Last night my friend Danny took me with him to buy about eight ounces of cocaine from some people we both knew from Santa Cruz. We met in the basement of a beautiful Spanish-style house in Beverly Hills. The sellers were two sons of a prominent Beverly Hills surgeon. One of them, the one with the wispy beard, was twenty. The other, the one with the greasy hair down to his shoulders, was nineteen. They had their own quarters down there, near the swimming pool. "Our parents can't hassle us down here," the bearded one said. "We can do our thing."

"We get our head together down here," the sideburned one said.

"I'm hip," I said.

From the stairs, a voice came. "Sean, you have not had dinner yet."

It was a mother's voice. Vaguely reproachful.

"Up in a minute, Mom," Sean said.

My friend Danny, seeking to expedite the process so that Sean could eat, said, "Hey, it's cool. I'll test it when I get home. No problem."

He picked up the plastic bag full of white powder and put it on a scale. It weighed exactly eight ounces. "It looks groovy to me," he said, with a big smile.

Danny handed Sean an envelope. "There's twelve thousand in there," he said. "You can count it."

Sean started to count the hundred-dollar bills. Then his

mother's voice came down the stairs again. "Sean," she said, "the chicken is getting cold, and Juanita wants to go to her room."

"O.K., Mom," Sean said. He turned to Danny. "Hey, man, I'll count it later. I know you're cool."

Later, in Danny's broken-down car, I asked him what if the cocaine was cut? What would he do if it were really stepped on?

"That won't happen," Danny said. "Sean and I are old friends. He wouldn't do that." He smiled under the light of a billboard on Sunset Strip as we headed back to Hollywood. "We went to elementary school together. My mom's a good friend of his mom."

Danny wants me to join him in the cocaine trade. I do not think I will. My mother does not have the connections that Danny's mother has.

November 18, 1976

I have not heard from my friend Sybil for a few days. She came over recently and started to do my dishes while I was out walking the dog. That is her form of repentance for having made anti-Semitic comments. That won't last. I told her to stop washing my dishes and stop saying the anti-Semitic remarks. For some reason, that offended her.

"You intimidate me," she said. Her eyes were so freighted with emotion that they actually sparkled, in a dim room, with her anger. It excited me, but nothing below the waist was allowed.

So I have not heard from her for a while. She is probably out collecting signatures against an oil refinery in a poor neighborhood along with one of her fellow heiresses. Her life mystifies me. There is so little in it, on the surface. There does not seem to be much in it under the surface too.

I don't mind not hearing from her, though. I am getting sick of her innuendos. She should have been a U.S. Senator. Between her money and the girl with the blue-green eyes' search for spiritual nurture, I will take the spiritual nurture anytime, even if it makes me plastic.

November 19, 1976

A snatch of conversation overheard at my office. Two secretaries to one another:

"I know he's married, but he's so sexy-looking, with that beard and that Porsche and that boat."

"I know."

"Even so, I just can't get it on with him, you know what I mean?"

"I know."

"I was in his office last week and we were taking each other's clothes off, you know?"

"I know."

"And I was ready and everything until I saw his underpants."

"Really."

"They were bikinis with a map of Hawaii on them. What could I do?"

"For sure."

November 20, 1976

Yesterday I felt like eating at home. The girl with blue-green eyes said she would like to cook dinner for me at home. "To show you what real food tastes like," she said.

She arrived at my apartment around 5 P.M. with two huge brown paper sacks. From one she hauled glittering cookware. From the other she pulled beautiful packages revealing nothing. "Just go into the living room and watch television," she said. "I want you to know what real food is like." While I watched the news, she poked her head out to tell me that she had to go to three different stores to get this "real" food. "One was in Santa Monica; one was in West L.A. and one was in North Hollywood," she said. I figured she drove close to fifty miles to get this "natural" food.

At about 7 P.M., she told me to come into the dining room. Dinner was ready.

On my plate was a lump of unrecognizable "natural" food. She pointed at part of the lump. "That's chicken," she said. "It's *real* chicken. It didn't sit in a shed getting fat. It wandered around a yard eating corn."

The "natural" chicken was a scrawny, miserable lump that had an off taste. It did not really even look like chicken. I diplomatically put it to the side.

"It's important," she said, "to eat natural foods. It's going to help save the environment. We have only a forty-five-day stockpile of food on this planet," she added, making me wonder what the stockpile was on other planets, whether it is accurate to call a food "natural" if you have to drive fifty miles to get it in the middle of a city, and what I was doing there.

Before that incident, many women offered to show me

what "real" food tastes like. I shine it on, as we say here. I should have yesterday. Southern California continues to spawn legions of "natural" food addicts, and some day I suppose there will be fast "real" food places on Ventura Boulevard. What then?

November 21, 1976

By a wonderful series of lucky breaks, I will earn a decent living this year. So I want to know how to pay my income taxes. Even though I took advanced tax in law school, and even though I understand fiscal policy, I hate doing my income tax. So I went to see Mike W., an accountant. He came highly recommended by the folks at the studio.

"A regular thief," they said. "He'll see that you don't pay a cent." With a recommendation like that, I rushed off to see Mike.

He is a short, amiable fellow, apparently adjusting to wearing contact lenses. He sat in a chair that the Sun King would have envied, behind a desk Charles de Gaulle would have liked if he could have afforded it. On a pad of yellow paper he wrote down my earnings as I listed them. It added up to what I thought was a princely annual figure.

He looked up at me, squinting slightly. "What about the second quarter?" he asked.

After I had picked up my composure, we went over my deductions. He knew about deductions I had not dreamed of. There was something almost salacious about all those deductions. I was not going to have to pay anywhere near as much tax as I had thought. Heaven.

While we talked, a tall, thin black man wearing a leather vest walked in. He was handed a power of attorney by Mike, which he obediently signed. "I think this will make things a lot easier," Mike said, and the black man nodded agreement.

When the man in the leather vest had left, I asked what

71

it was about. "I'm his business manager," Mike said. "It makes life a lot simpler."

"Should I have a business manager?" I asked.

"Maybe when you make some money," Mike said.

November 22, 1976

This evening, while I was talking with the girl with blue-green eyes, I was visited by my rich friend Sybil. She was obviously flustered that I had company. She tried to make polite conversation, which she had probably heard other people do, but she had no idea of how to do it. So she fidgeted for a while and then she left. I have no idea of why she came by.

After she had gone, the girl with blue-green eyes looked over at the place where she had sat and shook her head. I did not have to ask what she meant. Whoever made that money laid a curse on Sybil so strong that she will never be free.

I cannot think about it. I have my own life to make. There is no reward on earth, and none, I suspect, in heaven, for helping to psychoanalyze an heiress. It is better for everyone for me to simply go on with my dreams and for her to go on with her fantasies. That is why we are both in L.A.

November 23, 1976

At dinner tonight, a group of friends talked about how their careers were going. We listened to a vivacious, young-looking redhead who said she had just gotten a part in a low-budget movie called *West Coast Van Ladies*. She plays a nymphomaniac who likes to ball in vans more than anything.

"I say things like: 'Think those springs can take it, big boy?' " she said. She was happy about getting the part.

Another girl at the table was envious. "How the hell did you get that part, Cindy?" she asked.

Cindy looked proud. "My uncle's the producer and my mom just drove him crazy until he gave me the part," she said.

November 25, 1976

My birthday. I am thirty-two. My mother called and wanted to know how I was earning my living. I did not want to go into a long discussion with her, but I told her it was all right. I was making out O.K.

Sometimes I wonder myself. Then I think of all the things I do. I work for Norman Lear, although I enjoy it so much I can hardly call it working. I write articles, which I do not enjoy as much. I have contracts to do several books. And yet it does not feel as if I am working. That is a big difference from my work as a lawyer or a newspaper writer. Then, I spent a great deal of time doing things I hated, following rules that made no sense, all to please someone farther up the bureaucratic ladder. The goal was always to please someone and not to produce anything. At the FTC, my superiors were embarrassed by my volume of work. Now I have no superiors. I can produce as much as I want. The more the better. That makes sense to me.

That way, I can earn as much as I like, not as little as someone else likes. To me, that's Hollywood. No rules, except do what you can for yourself.

November 27, 1976

This afternoon I went to look at houses. We are having a hysterical housing boom here, such as one might imagine in a crumbling banana republic, and almost everything I see is far beyond my means. Still, I keep looking. There is something delicious about going into people's houses and seeing how they live. Giant fish tanks in the middle of living rooms, hidden cork-lined torture rooms, indoor pools for totally private water sports, and even a few places that looked like normal people had lived in them. I can forget about those.

The woman who took me around this afternoon was a friendly person about my age, with dark curly hair and big eyes that blinked constantly. After we looked at a few overpriced dumps, she asked me if I was doing anything more that afternoon.

"No," I said. "Do you have some more houses for me to see?"

"Not exactly," she said. "But I do have some good dope." Was it a come-on?

It was just what it sounded like.

A few hours later, she told me why she was selling real estate. "I started out at USC," she said. "I was going to be a biologist." She took a long hit on her joint. "Then I found out about balling." She giggled. "So I dropped out. All I could think of was balling, so I couldn't study."

It made a lot of sense.

November 28, 1976

Dinner last night with the girl with blue-green eyes at Perino's. That restaurant is far south on Wilshire Boulevard, in a neighborhood of wealthy Gentiles completely out of the Hollywood scene. They come and go from an enclave called Hancock Park, a region of homes with grassy lawns and houses set far back from the street. Ford station wagons and Cadillacs in the driveways tell me that it is a neighborhood of solid citizens. There are no Jaguars or Mercedeses here. None of the marks of those who have just made it yesterday. This is old, well-rolled, long-sanitized money.

At Perino's, the captain ushered us into a large room that looked like it had been taken lock, stock, and barrel, from a set of an M-G-M movie. The dining room was a large oval, well lit by chandeliers in the center of the room, with crystal coming down in streamers across the two halves of the oval. Semicircular padded booths lined the walls. Other round and square tables stood out in the center of the oval. Every man in the room wore a tie, which I had not seen since I came to L.A.

The men and women had a weary, sexually deprived look. Their clothes were unfashionable ten years ago. Yet they had a certain bearing I liked. They have seen the show business geniuses come and go, and they still cut their own lawns.

The men looked young and eager and well trimmed, but not too well trimmed. Their wives, as the girl with blue-green eyes said, "are the kind who order a Perfect Old Fashioned or a Rob Roy."

The diners looked at me. It made me uncomfortable. Hollywood is not really a part of Los Angeles, although

I love them both. The people at Perino's looked like the people at the *Wall Street Journal,* only more prosperous. I did not want to have to think about them and I did. I will not go there again.

For once the girl with blue-green eyes and I agreed.

"They're just plastic jerks," she said. "Who needs them?"

I nodded.

"You don't need them," she said. "You get more done in a week than they do in a year."

That was a new line from her and it made me wonder.

November 29, 1976

Last night I went to a party down the hall. The people were losers by almost any standard. That must have included me, or else why was I there? I talked to a tall girl with brown eyes and brown hair. She was not quite pretty, but extremely lively. We went over to my apartment and talked for a while.

After an hour, I went to the bathroom. When I came out, Wendy was not in the living room. There was a rustling from the bedroom. No lights. Through the window came the reflected light of Sunset Strip. Wendy was under the covers. She was not wearing anything I could see.

"What's going on?" I asked. I am a master of romance.

"Hush," she whispered. "Just come to bed."

I did as told. As I slid under the covers, she kissed and caressed me, and then held her right forefinger over her mouth. "Don't say anything," she said. She kissed me down my chest, almost to my navel. She looked up at me, her eyes just visible by the light from the window. "Tell me really," she sighed, "can you get me in to see Norman Lear?"

"Yes, I can," I said, "but only if you leave me alone for a few minutes. I'll meet you back at the party."

She left and I went out to the beach to spend the night with the girl with the blue-green eyes.

November 30, 1976

Sometimes I ride along La Brea Avenue in my car and I turn off onto Franklin and then go down one of the small streets like Camino Palmiero or Sierra Bonita and look at the small Spanish houses, the small deco houses, the small bungalows—houses that look like whimsy in concrete—and I wonder how I could be so lucky. The sun pours down on the streets and through my sun roof onto my head, and I look around me at the sidewalks with the girls in tight jeans and T-shirts and I feel like singing.

Everything—the car, the houses, the girls, the sun, the balmy air, the palm trees, the ocean—everything—the studio, the glib talk, the self-promotion, most of all, the writing—has a sharp, frictionless quality. Life here goes on without any drag. There is nothing of the slowed-down, drawn-out feeling of life I felt in other cities. Daily life cuts cleanly through the mind. There is no gritty feeling about doing anything here.

And, because of that, it all takes on a dreamlike quality. Even sitting at home with a friend who is completely into daytime quiz shows, as I sometimes do, has a clean, exhilarating quality.

It all has something to do with dreams. I noticed for a long time before I came here that the best part of my life was when I was dreaming. Dreams are never boring or dull. I never said to myself that I wished this dream would be over because it was so wearing. Sometimes the dreams were frightening, but never a bother, never dull. That is life in L.A. It has an effortless, floating quality about it, like the unreal houses, that is more or less pure pleasure. Life in L.A. is like the dreaming without the nightmares.

December 1, 1976

This morning the head of my studio and a few producers and I kicked around a few ideas about new story lines. I told them I thought there should be one story about a rich liberal, almost a socialist, who spends a lot of time trying to get himself into tax shelters and avoid paying any income tax, even though he talks about equality a lot.

The studio head and the producers stared at me.

"What's funny about that?" the studio head asked.

December 3, 1976

Last night my friend M., a woman editor of a major news-magazine, took me to dinner at the home of her friend Leon, a young, superbig producer. His home was a huge "Jewish-Chinese" monstrosity in Bel Air. Outside, it looked tasteless and horrible. Inside, it was exactly to my taste, with large rooms and wide windows. African art and German "objets d'art" were everywhere. It was a wonderful house with sweeping views out over the city. After dinner, we sat at round tables around the pool, while Filipinos served brandy.

It was a stupendous sight. Below the sparkling blue waters of the pool were an infinitude of L.A. lights, arranged in neat grids stretching away toward the ocean, where they stopped abruptly. Around my table were the biggest names on the Hollywood A list: Peter Duchin, with wife Cheray; Billy Wilder, with wife Audrey; Freddie de Cordova (producer of *The Tonight Show*), with wife Janet. She, although in late middle age, was still beautiful. She told me about life at the Mocambo and Ciro's when she used to see Clark Gable there. It all sounded glamorous.

Someone took out a gold chain purse, took out a gold cigarette case, took out reefers, and started to pass them around. Not everyone smoked. It was not top-grade smoke. I suspect that the kids in Compton get better dope.

Back in the living room, Sue Mengers, David Geffen and a producer of spectacular movies were laughing. My friend M. started to argue with the producer about something. A Filipino waiter decorously served more drinks.

"I think you don't realize exactly what your movies look like when they're in a small theater without a gigantic screen," my friend said. "I think you should think about that. I really do," she said.

The producer, bushy-haired hippie type, son of a deceased movie star, said, with a trace of an accent, "I think you're a dumb cunt."

December 4, 1976

After endless searching, I found a house I like and can afford. It's high up in the Santa Monica Mountains, which run through the middle of this city, and it looks down over the San Fernando Valley on one side and the city on the other side. I love it. It is owned by a frightening-looking guy named Frankie, who has the house decorated with obscene love couches and revolting sparkles in the bedroom ceiling. I love it. I knew that Frankie and I were kindred spirits when I saw the furniture. Distinctively rented.

In a few months I will move in. That will be a thrill. The first house I owned, in Washington, was an old Dutch colonial in a fancy neighborhood. But the house itself was a mess. The people who lived near me in Washington were always outside, gardening. They were lovely people. All the children went to Saint Albans or Sidwell Friends.

In my new neighborhood, there aren't any children, and people go outside mainly to start their cars.

Not me. My backyard will have palm trees and roses and a giant eucalyptus tree and century plants, and I love it already. I will sit in it and remember when I lived in New York and wanted to sit outside and had no place to sit.

And I will remember when a palm tree of my own was just a dream.

December 6, 1976

Here is what happens when your Mercedes starts to act up: My car made a clicking noise as I turned around a corner. I slowed down to listen. Then I turned off the radio. Disaster! The aerial, which is supposed to go down automatically, paused defiantly, quiveringly, halfway down.

Trembling with fear, I called Beverly Hills Mercedes. I told the "service consultant" my problem.

He breathed slowly. "Sounds serious," he said, with a heavy German accent.

"Can I bring it in right away?"

"You haff to make an appointment. Let me put on my secretary," he said.

I made an appointment for the next morning.

At the immaculate service department, white-coated men with straight blond hair hurried back and forth carrying charts, like doctors at a major teaching hospital. Kurt, my service consultant, gravely studied the problem. All around me, frightened and nervous owners paced back and forth while the men in white probed their cars. There was a waiting area with a pot of coffee.

"Vee shall haff to keep it all day," Kurt said.

"How much will it cost?" I asked.

Kurt looked at me sadly. "Vee cannot say at zis time," he said. "But it vill not be more than five hundred dollars."

I was in deep shock all day. At about 3 P.M., Kurt called. His voice was weary, like a surgeon after performing major and life-threatening surgery. "It is finished," he said.

"How much will I have to pay?" I asked.

He referred me to his secretary, who cheerily told me that it would be only two hundred and seventy dollars.

I picked up my repaired car, happily paid up, and left. Behind the wheel of my Mercedes, I felt proud that I had the money to spend like water on a mere car. Just the fact that it costs so much shows what a great car it is, and just the fact that I did it without fainting shows how brave I am.

But even so, the Germans are clearly winning that war.

December 8, 1976

As I looked around at the Palm at lunchtime today, I had the sinking feeling that everyone was getting ahead, while I was stuck behind, laboriously writing, instead of making deals. My friend Mike, a hustler, sat across from me, shirt open to his waist, munching on salad, telling me that this person has made a million and that person has made a million, and it got me down. Where is my million?

"You have to have a racket, man," Mike said. "There's no way you can do it just sitting at your desk, jerking off."

I thought it was useless to tell him that not all writing was jerking off. He had a point.

Mike had an opportunity for us to get rich. A man who owned a company that manufactured sex aids wanted to sell.

"It's a sweet shot," he said. "Definitely looking good." The man manufactured dildos, both black and white, plastic vaginas "with real hair, no shit," and other items. He had a little plant in downtown L.A., and we could inspect it and the books at any time. If I put up most of the money, Mike said, he would run the business and sell the stuff and give me half the profits.

"This is our chance," Mike said. "There's no telling how big this thing could be."

"Really," I said.

When I got home, I thought about it. *"Non olet,"* they say, and yet something in my mind resents the whole idea. Even in L.A., you can get turned around by what you do. I considered becoming an investment banker at one time. I could have done it. But I decided it was not interesting enough. Is manufacturing dildos what I want to do? Does it change the kind of person I am?

Just asking these questions, Mike says, is what makes a person a schmuck.

December 9, 1976

California kids, at least the ones who belong to successful Hollywood couples, are a race apart. The word "spoiled" does not do justice to them. "Indolent," "self-centered," "manipulative," "whining," "irritable," "mocking" and "ignorant" go part of the way, but there is a lot more to be said. A bored, contemptuous look appears on their face at an early age, and is only wiped away when their parents stop supporting them, which can be a long time.

This all came up at a dinner party last night. My friends the C.'s, who had the party, were complaining mildly about their daughter. A woman across the table took up the lament. "Jason just dropped out of school to find himself," she said. The father chimed in, "When he does find himself, he'll throw up for three weeks."

A few minutes later, the woman asked another man how his "active boy, Doug," was getting along.

"He's not quite as active now," the father said, a note of glee in his voice. "He's in the UCLA Med Center psychiatric ward." He looked pleased.

December 12, 1976

Last night Sybil and I went to Mifune, a Japanese restaurant in West L.A. Sybil and I sat in the dark café talking about why she needs a job. I talked to her with great enthusiasm for over an hour. She was still undecided when I had finished. On a formica counter next to where we sat, a huge roach crawled toward Sybil's fleecy arm. At the last moment, I warned her. She jerked her arm up, knocking over her Kirin beer. She gave a little howl, and the waitress came over, muttering in Japanese, to wipe up after Sybil and the cockroach.

After dinner, we went back to Sybil's house to do a little dope. Sybil looked worried until it hit her. Then her face relaxed and she looked calm and beautiful. After a while, she became almost a new person. Then she started to fall asleep, and I left.

I drove down the long hill from her house to Sunset Boulevard. The old-fashioned street lights cast the trees into soft shadow. Walled Spanish-style houses lined the street. On the radio, Janis Joplin was still alive, asking me to take a piece of her heart. L.A. is almost too good to be true. I don't know why. It has nothing to do with Sybil. It has something to do with the old-fashioned lamps and the Spanish-style houses.

December 13, 1976

A trip into the desert with the girl with blue-green eyes. I have never been into the desert before, and this was a treat. We headed for Palm Springs.

For over an hour, we drove through the sprawl of Los Angeles and its satellites: Pasadena, West Covina, Fontana (where the McDonald's is), Colton, San Bernardino, Banning. Miserable scenery of mobile homes and small factories.

Then, as abruptly as the change from one backyard to another, there is the desert. The green grass and trees stop suddenly, and the sagebrush and cactus begin, not quite covering over the baked, harsh earth. Wind blows the dust and mesquite in swirls in the hot air. Beyond the road, mountains which look like no other mountains I have seen loom up, craggy, raw, angry, utterly without vegetation, slag heaps thrown down to earth by disgusted gods.

There are many billboards advertising hotels and housing developments in booming Palm Springs. The Cadillacs and campers speed by, throwing up sand in front of the lavish country club estates near Bob Hope Drive.

Palm Springs is jammed. In the middle of nowhere is a traffic jam with a few stores on either side. Old people, looking happy and eager, line the streets, chewing on fudge from white bags.

The sun is blinding, even with tinted glass, even with sunglasses. When I stepped out of the car to ask for directions, I thought I would lose my mind.

At the hotel, thin, wealthy, relaxed people glide by, in tennis outfits and woven golf clothes.

At night, in the sky over the mountains, lightning flashes

and thunder rolls across the desert to our room. We sit on the balcony in our pajamas, in the dark, watching the sky, until the girl with blue-green eyes starts to cry.

"It's just so beautiful," she says, and it is.

All night long, the lightning casts blue-white light and gray shadows on the bed.

December 14, 1976

We have been taking pictures for the book about *Mary Hartman.*

This afternoon we used a gorgeous blond model from New Zealand. We dressed her up as a schoolgirl, as a disciplinarian, as a Nazi. She looked wonderful in every outfit.

At the end of the shooting, I told the girl, a magnificent creature, that I hoped she understood it was all in fun. "Don't feel bad about the costumes we made you wear. It's for a funny book."

She looked at me quizzically. "Are you kidding?" she asked. "I should have paid you."

I have to get that girl's telephone number right away.

December 15, 1976

Here is how you get into the cocaine business. A friend offers to double my money in a month if I will lend him enough money to buy a few ounces. He will buy three ounces for $3,500. Each ounce has about thirty grams. That adds up to ninety grams. He will sell them for one hundred dollars each. Some will fall through the lines and some will be snorted and some will not be sold for one hundred dollars a gram. But that is the principle. What about the law?

"The cops don't hassle people doing grams," my friend said. "They're too busy with the people doing pounds."

All I would have to do is put up the money, and I could have the title of his car as collateral.

It is exactly what I do not want to do, in every way.

December 17, 1976

A visit to a girl I went to high school with, back in Silver Spring, Maryland. She has gotten to be emaciated and sarcastic. I picked her up at her modest apartment in West L.A. She stared at my car but did not say anything. That was all right. It was just the same as if she did say something.

How had I done so well? She kept asking me that. There were two answers. First, she greatly exaggerated how well I had done. Second, I don't know. What was Norman Lear like? Could she get a job at Tandem? How had I done so well? Again and again, like a tape loop. At the end of the dinner, I walked her back to her apartment door and offered a firm handshake, which was more than I wanted to do. She grasped my head and kissed me as if it would make her rich. Could I come into her apartment for a while? Did I have to get up early the next day? No and yes.

And still, I thought as I drove away, no comment on my car. She knows nothing about life in L.A. If she knew anything, she would have said something about the car.

December 20, 1976

I do not need to see Sybil anymore. I ran into her on Sunset Boulevard. She pulled her car over and we talked. She told me that her mother had just gone home from a five-day visit.

"She really liked my friends," Sybil said.

"What the hell am I?" I asked as the traffic flew by.

Sybil looked worried. "I mean old friends from a long time," Sybil said.

"Jesus Christ," I said. "Don't you think I would have liked to meet her?"

Sybil glared at me. "I didn't know you were so big on etiquette," she said.

"Is that why you didn't introduce me to your mother? Because of etiquette?"

Of course Sybil does not need to answer. And further, of course, it is very un-L.A. of me to even think about it very much. It is uncool to worry very much about what other people do or say. One of my friends here might say that it does not apply. But it does if it hurts.

Tonight I saw the girl with blue-green eyes. She takes away the pain and gives me shelter. Doing, not thinking, is salvation in L.A.

January 11, 1977

Sometimes when I think of my friend Al and his wife, Sally, tears come to my eyes. I met them when I was in Aspen, Colorado, at a conference about television. Al is a creative boss at my studio. All the other participants were academics and journalists, sneering at Al and drooling at how much money he made. Their envy became truly ugly. It was a vivid and frightening scene of those who teach venting their jealousy on those who do.

I tried to be supportive to Al, even though I dislike most of his TV shows. I admire people who get things done. Sally, Al's wife, is perhaps the most intense woman I have ever met, but she was perfectly nice to me.

By encouraging me about finding work here, they made it possible for me to move here. I do not think that there are better friends anywhere. Where, I wonder, have friends like them been all my life? They are almost completely unfrustrated people. If they want to do something, they simply do it. No agonizing, no whimpering, no brooding— they just do it.

In a way, they are L.A. for me. Everything is out there, on the surface. Nothing below it counts. Maybe there is nothing below it. It does not matter if there is. Sometimes I think I would like to spend my life in Al's office, listening to him wheeling and dealing, always straightforward, always without animosity. I love them, Al and Sally. They are L.A.

When I remember all the deep thinkers I have known who cannot be bothered, and Al and Sally, who can never do enough, I wonder if I should have gone into the garment business, or somewhere that had people who could get their heads out of their asses. In L.A., I have learned, getting things done means more than every brilliant aperçu that ever was.

January 12, 1977

In Paris you fall in love. In Boston you go to school. In L.A. you hustle. And you try to become beautiful.

My friend Marge and I went out to a steak place for dinner last night.

Mike the hustler made the reservation. "It's so exclusive," he said, "that you have to make a reservation, and even then, if the owner doesn't like you, you don't get in."

The restaurant is a miserable, dingy dive on a deserted, gloomy street. A customer would be lucky if the owner didn't like him.

Mike's wife is Lenore. She wants to be an actress, but she's been working in a boutique. She's a pretty girl with an Irish face and flowing red hair. More than pretty—beautiful.

"Ben," Mike says, "I have gotten into the best thing I've ever gotten into. The best." He smiles around the table. "I figure to make ten million next year." Gasps. "I am going to get the exclusive franchise to sell Red Chinese ginseng root." I looked blank. I did not know what ginseng root was. No courses on ginseng root in law school.

Mike points suggestively at his crotch. "You know what ginseng root does, don't you? It juices you up, if you know what I mean."

I look like I get it, even though I have read that there is no such thing as a chemical aphrodisiac.

"The stuff they sell here is Korean ginseng root," Mike says. "It stinks." He holds his nose as if there were a bad smell in the room. "But that Korean shit sold seventy-five million last year. I figure that the Chinese stuff will sell a hundred million, easy, and I get ten percent."

Big money in health foods, everyone at the table agrees. Major bucks. "Really," everyone says.

Lenore looks bored. She holds out her hand and looks at it. "I started the Laszlo beauty treatment," she says. It's a treatment sold at Saks and other stores for the care of the skin. It involves washing the face fifty times a day, among other things. "It's hard work," Lenore says, "but it's worth it. It's changed my life."

Appreciative nods.

Marge says that she is sick of her name. She wants a new name. I suggest Margaret Devere.

"I like the Devere part," she says, "but I'm not sure about the Margaret."

The woman next to me suggests Margot Devere.

It is a sensation. It catches on at once.

Talk turns to Jacuzzis. "I don't know about Laszlo," the woman next to me says, "but my Jacuzzi has changed my life."

This morning Mike called to ask for something. I asked him how the ginseng root business was.

"Oh, forget that," he says. "The guy never called me back."

Later today I called Marge at the real estate office where she works. When she picked up the phone she said, without knowing it was I on the line, "Margot Devere. May I help you?"

January 15, 1977

Brunch at the home of a production designer. A young directress, a young producer and I make up the group. The directress has temporarily finished working on *Audrey Rose*, a new movie about reincarnation. The conversation goes something like this.

DIRECTESS: A lot of people think that if a kid died violently, he comes back sooner, and since so many kids died in World War Two, that's why so many kids were born in the baby boom after World War Two.

PRODUCER: I know a lot of people think that, but I'm not sure. I think maybe when you come back depends on what you come back as.

DESIGNER: That's what I've always thought.

DIRECTRESS: Well, I know that's what most people think, but I think my theory makes a lot of sense. How else do you explain all those kids being born after World War Two?

PRODUCER: It could be because so many other animals were killed and they came back as humans.

DIRECTRESS: Maybe, but you've got to explain it somehow, and my theory makes a lot of sense. But you're right. Your theory is what most people think.

Luckily, the conversation completely avoided any mention of family formation, or the social effects of war, or any of those explanations which are not what most people think.

There is something in the air here which encourages what I would call bizarre explanations for everything, as well as bizarre attempts to find solutions. At the studio where I work, all major national and international events are explained as manifestations of the CIA's conspiracy. At a party, a woman introduced me to a man and said, "Roger's the one who first explained to me about the CIA and the multinationals. I hadn't understood about them at all before now."

The discouraging thing is that I have started to believe in the CIA as villain too. A few days ago, someone meaningfully told me a rumor that Richard Helms, long-time director of the CIA, had begun his career in 1936 as a reporter in Germany. This piece of data made sense only as evidence of his deep complicity in CIA-Multinationals-Nazi plotting, which people here believe in absolutely. The belief is so pervasive, so completely certain, that it is easier to roll with the punch and simply start believing in CIA plots too. Plus, it passes the time.

It doesn't matter that I have worked in the bureaucracy and know that almost everything can be explained by simple incompetence and bureaucratic buck-passing. The tide here is so strongly in favor of conspiracy that facts and real knowledge are simply impediments to finding a niche.

Having worked for Nixon, even in a very minor capacity, makes me the center of attention for conspiracy theorists, which means everyone.

"When is he making his comeback?"

"What's it like at San Clemente?"

"How much did Nixon steal?"

"Why would the CIA do it to Nixon, of all people?"

Some of the theories are more elaborate: "Just follow Alexander Haig, and you'll understand everything."

Exotic explanations for everything hang in the air, like the hydrangea that blooms year round.

When I first came here, I wanted to teach a class in the political content of film. Compared to the bureaucracy at UCLA, the federal bureaucracy is like greased lightning.

After a while a friend referred me to the Center for the Healing Arts. "It has a lot of very devoted students," she said, handing me the catalogue.

The catalogue described courses such as "Sexual Energetics," "Psychoenergetics and Interaction," "The Drama of Energy Transmission Through Human Participation" and "Dream Energetics." My favorite was a Thursday-evening class entitled "The Closeness of Wholeness":

> There is an intuitive process that is ever beckoning each one of us to move into a relationship with life which yields to us experiences which include joy, peace and happiness, and which yields to live *all that we are*. . . . Finally, oneness, the encounter with *the always you, the all ways you*, will be achieved. *IT* will be understood. The workshop process will involve meditations, movements, and various energies, individual and group, and articulations.
>
> [The teacher] is a lifelong student of the intuitive process. He has become increasingly focused on the way in which he can share all that he is with all that life is. . . . His life also includes many years of professional engineering work and many lifetimes of poetic expressiveness.

The woman who gave me the catalogue told me that at her daughter's private day school, there had been a psychological counselor who was a doctor. Only after a year of experimental counseling was it learned that he was a veterinarian. He now has a private practice in counseling, somewhere in the San Fernando Valley.

Down the hall from me at the studio is an adorable cutie named Yolande. One day last week I saw her filling out an application for postgraduate training at est.

"You know," she said to me, "before I took est, my whole life was just wasted. Now I can get through the worst crisis, or what someone else would call a crisis, without it bothering me at all."

"Terrific," I said.

"Really," she said.

"When's the postgraduate course?" I asked.

"As soon as I can get thirty dollars together," she said. "Money's hard to come by these days, you know," she added.

"Really," I said.

A friend here has been through Arica, est, Rolfing, Sufi and Tantric yoga. Now his plan is to rent an ice cream truck and sell ice cream outside a private girls' school here. He wants me to be his partner. I think I will. In fact, I'd better call him right away.

January 21, 1977

Yesterday morning I had surgery of medium dimensions for a medium problem. It was the first surgery I have had since I was six years old. A year ago, I had an automobile accident while briefly visiting in Hollywood, and I went to a hospital emergency room. It was so neat and the nurses so friendly that I said to myself that if I ever had to have surgery, I hoped it would be in L.A., and so it was.

I woke up hours before the time of the operation and sat in a chair smoking cigarettes. My hospital was and is in Santa Monica. My room looked out over a row of palm trees and a patch of ocean. The room itself has rounded windows, 1940s modern.

I wondered if an evil spirit had made me have the operation, and a good spirit had made it happen in Los Angeles. I loved seeing that ocean, even knowing that I would soon be under the knife. L.A. will heal me, I thought. Now I am recovering, they say, and I can still see the ocean.

Roxanne called and asked me, with a giggle, if there was anything she could do for me. My parents were in the room, so I told her I would talk to her later. How can anyone live anywhere else?

January 22, 1977

Mike came to visit me in the hospital this evening. He and I talked for a long time about what I might do if I sell some screen rights and get together a little bit of money. He gave me this Hollywood fiscal advice:

"Get one of those really big houses in the flats of Beverly Hills. Put down as little as you can. Pay for it on credit. Then get a big second mortgage and buy a Rolls-Royce convertible."

I love it. Personal finance, Hollywood style. I felt so good after that advice that I didn't need any painkiller tonight.

January 28, 1977

Los Angeles, John Mankiewicz says, is completely now and totally happening. Whenever I tell that to someone, he always asks what it means.

Today was a completely now and totally happening day, at least for a while. I went to lunch at the Palm with a producer named Mark Feinman. The Palm is where hustling young producers and writers gather. The food is greasy, but producers like it. I love it. The best steak on earth is sold there. I used to think it was greasy, but now I am addicted. The last time I was there, the fellow I ate with said that he loved the Palm because it reeks "of this business we're in, this entertainment business." He, in fact, is in the business of selling funeral plots over the telephone and is just one step ahead of the Federal Trade Commission.

But Mark Feinman really is a producer. He has the wrist jewelry and the hairy chest to prove it. He also carries a little pocketbook. He has gotten hooked up to a Chicago financier who has so much money "that losing a million for him is like losing fifty for you and me."

He's interested in my novel. He hasn't seen the galleys, but he loves the idea. He loves it. It's terrific. Very commercial. Sort of like *The Towering Inferno*. When can he see the galleys? Anytime, I say. My agent should have sent them already. He also likes my idea for a movie about a teen-age girl and a middle-aged man having an affair. "Very major box office potential," he says, "if it's handled right."

Across the aisle from us sits Brooke Hopper, a beautiful woman whose book about her parents, Leland Hayward and Margaret Sullavan, has just been sold to a paperback house for over $300,000. The last time I saw her I paid for her meal, which now seems funny. She comes over and rubs my head. "Where have you been, Ben?" she asks, as if I were a relative. "Where the hell have you been?"

I congratulate her and she asks, "For what?"

For the money, I say.

She makes a face as if to say that it's nothing. "Listen," she says, "how about taking me to dinner next week?"

Fine, I say. You pay. She laughs.

When Mark Feinman learns who she is, he's impressed. That's part of being totally happening.

I drive Mark Feinman back to his office. "Listen," he says, "we've got the money and we're ready to go. Check on those galleys, will you?"

I drive home in a soft rain. The rain here is so soft that it's more like a mist, like stepping out of the shower.

My answering service tells me that Norman Lear has called. I call him back, since I like him and I work for him. He wants to know how I'm feeling, since I just had an operation. "I just wanted to check on you out of pure affection," he says, "nothing else." He's an affectionate person. He also wants to know Joan Didion's telephone number.

Then I call my agent. Why hasn't Mark Feinman gotten the galleys? The secretary doesn't know. Things don't go too fast when they're sent book rate, she says.

I cannot believe my ears. My agent has told me that a property like my novel could be worth hundreds of thousands, and they're sending it book rate to save thirty cents?

Book rate is not totally happening.

January 29, 1977

I am not yet recovered sufficiently to get myself into high writing form. That takes sitting at the typewriter and writing furiously for an hour at a time, and the operation took too much out of me for that.

I thought I would enjoy the change from my usual routine, but I miss it instead. Generally I sit at my desk and look out over the city as I make up whatever I am writing and put it down on the page. I set myself a certain number of pages to write or a certain scene to complete, and I feel wonderful if I can get it done.

Since I came to Los Angeles, I always get it done. And afterwards I always feel wonderful. Always. There is a kind of writer's euphoria about getting something out of your cobwebbed brain and down in black and white. I love it. It's like riding in my car. For a half hour after I finish, I lie in bed watching *Starsky and Hutch* or *The Streets of San Francisco*, and it's all there. Right there in the study next to my bedroom, it is all there.

January 30, 1977

Today while driving home from the studio I turned on my radio and heard, among other things, an advertisement for a certain "Dr. Frankel," who wanted to know why people in Los Angeles put up with looking the way they looked when they could look better. Dr. Frankel, a "credit doctor," told listeners that he could perform "tummy tucks, breast enlargement or reduction, face-lifts" and so forth. He especially recommended hair transplants for men. "All work," he said, "is done by skilled doctors and nurses in licensed hospitals." The advertisement added that the work is also tax deductible.

I looked at myself in the rear-view mirror and found much work for Dr. Frankel.

In Washington, I would not even have looked in the mirror.

January 31, 1977

While I was recuperating from my operation, my friend Debi visited me. She is a physicist and a religious fanatic. She is the only Orthodox Jew I have met since coming to L.A. She nags me constantly to go to services and light candles. She talks to me in Yiddish, as if to trick me into answering her in Yiddish. She will not believe that I do not know Yiddish. She is going on and on about people changing their names.

It made me think. At my office there is a beautiful girl named Estelle Duchamps DeVine. She was born, they say, Esther Dubinsky. It is hard to say what she has accomplished by the change. And yet it happens all the time. In my office we have Winthrops who are Jewish, Wellingtons one generation out of the shtetl, and Dillonses who still look like *yeshiva bochers*. Should I change my name? I don't think so. There is some limit to concessions, even concessions to L.A. I will have to ask Estelle if it's true that changed names have more fun.

But poor Debi, I thought. In L.A., no one wants to hear her theories about the artist and the merchant in Jewish culture. This is the city for doing, not thinking. This is where the Talmud is only useful if it could make a good series. I told Debi that she should move back to New York. She reminds me of old great-aunts in Upper West Side apartments. I think L.A. can be cruel to such people and I do not want to see her suffer.

February 4, 1977

I once considered Ma Maison an important and classy restaurant in Hollywood. Every night the small parking lot in front of the restaurant is filled with Mercedeses and Rolls-Royces. Lesser cars are parked across the street in a dark lot. The valet unsmilingly gets them when the owners come out.

Tonight I ate there with my former agent, David Obst, Al, and our wives or girl friends. A loudspeaker was blaring out heavy metal rock. I asked the owner if he could turn it down. "I am sorry," he said, "but it is impossible."

Quincy Jones came in about ten minutes later and made a similar request. Rubbing his hands together obsequiously, the owner turned off the radio. During the meal, I asked the waiter if the house white wine was all right.

"Zee house white wine," he said, bowing slightly, "eet ees the good trip."

That's another place I don't need to go to.

February 5, 1977

Today I moved into my new house. My wonderful maid, Sarah, a Czechoslovakian refugee, did almost all of the moving. The rented furniture people did the rest.

I never realized until tonight how windy Los Angeles was. I had read about it in Joan Didion's essays, but down on Sunset Strip I never felt it. Up here, the wind is terrifying. Great masses of hot air rush across Nevada, become hotter still, roar across the Mojave, break up over the San Gabriel Mountains, then regroup in the San Fernando Valley, charge up the canyons, intensifying their strength in the funnels of chaparral and granite, and smash against my house. The whole house shakes from the force.

Sarah and I sat in the living room and watched the trees bend in the wind. There was a fire burning in my fireplace and it was like camping out, as far as I know.

As one blast after another shook the house, Sarah said, "It's so," and she struggled for the word, "it's so existential."

February 6, 1977

The girl with blue-green eyes comes to visit me every day. She does not work, so she has plenty of time. She lives north of Malibu, in the hills above Trancas, in a cabin on a hillside overlooking the ocean. She writes at a laborious pace on her life story. She will not show it to me. Once I saw a snatch of it in her car. It said, "Today, no children will play. No birds will sing. No flowers will bloom." I wonder what that meant.

The girl with blue-green eyes wants to move in with me. In a way that would be good. She is a good influence. She hates drugs and likes clean living. She is neat and clean.

But there is something unfree about her which is in conflict with the whole idea of L.A. Within the open, boundless metropolis and archipelago of creativity, she lives in her own world of frustration and obsession. She does not skim along on the surface of life as she should. Instead, she wallows in some kind of problem underground. I love the girl with blue-green eyes, but a person has to be free, and my freedom is a delicate thing. I don't think it could survive living with someone in chains.

I told the girl with blue-green eyes that she could not move in with me.

"It's O.K.," she said. "I didn't really want to leave Malibu anyway." Then she told me about how her mother had always made her apologize even for having been born.

That is exactly the problem. Deep analysis is not L.A.

Still, I love her and I want her to know it. When I am completely recovered, I will try to do something to show her. I wish I could afford to buy a Mercedes for her. That would be love.

Instead, I told her that she had taught me a lot, and that even though she might think I was mocking her, I loved her and her soul too. "You keep me upright, in some way I could not tell you about even if I wanted to," I said.

She cried again. I sometimes wonder why I bother hanging around with anyone else. I love girls with blue-green eyes who are lonely and talk about their souls.

February 8, 1977

A meeting this morning with a major agent. Major. Really.
He is an elderly man, lying on a bed with a raised back.
Above him is a chin strap for traction. He is wearing
light-blue pajamas with a maroon scarf around his neck.
His telephone never stops ringing—calls from New York,
from Vegas, from everywhere.

He tells me that he has just made a major sale of a client's
book to a television network. "We got a hundred thousand
for it," he said, "which is major bucks for this kind of
thing."

I nod. "Really," I think to myself.

A call comes in on the agent's speakerphone. "Paul,"
the agent asks, the louveliers reflecting off his sunglasses
and the swimming pool reflecting off the louveliers, "when
are we going to get the money for the TV sale?" He is
talking about the same book. "It's supposed to be sixty
thousand." There is some haggling from the other end
and the agent says, "All right. Just send us thirty thousand
and we'll go to Brazil." Much laughter all around.

As he hangs up, the agent winks at me. "I got him to
give it all to us up front," he says. "These lawyers aren't
so smart."

Another call, this time from the head of a large paperback house in New York. Talk turns to the book, which
may have been sold for sixty thousand or a hundred thousand or thirty thousand.

"You dope," the agent says. "I offered you that book a
long time ago, and now it's going to be a big paperback
sale and it's going to Delacorte. We got a TV sale too.
Two hundred thousand up front."

At the end of the meeting, the agent takes my hand

and says, "Call me later. I think it's a viable package."

In the whole history of the world, there could hardly have been a more beautiful day than today. The sun was shining; the sky was clear and dry, and the temperature was perfect.

February 11, 1977

Dinner last night with the head of my studio. He is a famous man in this town and around the country. We ate at the Bistro, a well-known Beverly Hills watering hole, where everyone danced attendance upon him.

He is a Los Angeles phenomenon, to my way of thinking. He produces and partly writes nine television shows. He develops new television shows constantly. He gives speeches and receives awards. He is constantly producing, creating, inventing, getting things done.

I often try to study how he has gotten where he is, because I would like to imitate him. To some extent, he has something born deep within which tells him that anything is possible. He recognizes no limits on human potential. There are probably a few people born with that gift every year. In most occupations and parts of the world it would lie fallow. Here in L.A., where the entire ethos of life is that everything is doable, it sprouted, flourished and grew huge.

He is like some of the people I knew at the White House in that he is always confident, always sure of what he is doing. But as I talked to him at dinner tonight, I realized that there was more to it.

Those people at the White House were people whose strength derived from their rigidity. They were like great oaks, weathering the terrible gusts of Watergate until the final, most devastating gust from on high blew them down completely. They still operate and succeed, but few of them will ever be mighty again. Probably none of them.

The studio head is strong because he is flexible. He does not establish himself to dominate or to overbear. He listens and he adapts. He is a willow, adjusting to the wind and blossoming year after year, in every kind of weather. It is an L.A. quality.

It comes across in his personality. He could not possibly be less pompous. He makes me see the ridiculousness of the rest of the world.

There is something else about him, I realized tonight. He is always producing, gathering up material, digesting it, rearranging it in dramatic forms. He lives to create and to produce and for no other particular reason. In the land where everything depends on what you get done, he is king, because he can do the most. And he can do the most because it is not work for him. It is no less than life.

He produces more than television shows and money, though. He generates a way of life that is informed, cheerful and concerned. He acts good to me. He looks good. I have never heard him raise his voice to anyone and that example is followed throughout the studio. His life is his finest creation.

Perhaps if I had met someone like him in another city, I would have associated his type with another city. But I only met one person like him, and that was here in L.A. and it was he.

At the end of the dinner tonight, the girl with blue-green eyes said, he whispered in her ear that he was lucky to work with me. "He sees everything so clearly, so warmly," the studio head said. "He always cares what happens to people and that's more important than being smart."

I thought of him and of the bosses I have had in other jobs, men and women of such meanness, fear and jealousy that they would have been happy working for Beria, and I thank God I am where I am.

February 12, 1977

Baby oil is all right. So is cold cream. So is avocado oil. So is peanut oil. So is Kama Sutra love oil. But avoid that oil of menthol. If she has it in her hand, she is into something far kinkier than most people want to know about. Stick with something like K-Y.

Such are the lessons of L.A. life.

February 14, 1977

Valentine's Day. I sent flowers to my former wife, which was good, and to the girls at the studio, but I made a mistake. I gave Sarah, my maid, candy when she wanted flowers.

She left out on the coffee table a note saying: "Valentine's Day is the saddest day of the year." I felt terrible. Sarah is developing a crush on me, probably because she sees so few other people. But I must keep her at bay. I like her a lot, but she broods. That is not the way we do things here. No brooding.

Still, I felt guilty about it. That in itself was rare. I almost never feel guilty here. I do not know why, but there it is. No one tries to make me feel guilty, and I do not. Except for today.

February 20, 1977

The velvet alley. That is when you are making more money than you ever dreamed you would make, but are spending:
1. $250 a month on car payments;
2. $100 a month for car insurance;
3. $600 a month on restaurant meals you did not know you needed;
4. $700 a month on a housekeeper who is indispensable— and checks for $100 seem to flow out of the checkbook as if they had a life of their own.

"Don't even try to fight it," Al says. "You can't win. Anyway, what did you come here for?"

"Put in $400 for me," said the girl with blue-green eyes.

February 25, 1977

A Hollywood nightmare: My car is broken. Beverly Hills Mercedes charges me seven hundred dollars and does not fix it. Hollywood Mercedes charges me five hundred dollars and fixes it wrong. I take it from dealer to dealer and no one can fix it. I awake in a sweat. It was only a fantasy.

A Hollywood dream: On my way to the studio a few days ago, I pulled up next to a car from Illinois, a station wagon, with a mommy and daddy tourist and two children tourists. I sat in my car, windows rolled up, air conditioning on, stereo blasting, dark glasses over my eyes. I looked over at the tourists. The mommy's lips were saying, "He must be a movie star. Look at the car." She was pointing at me. This one really happened.

February 28, 1977

This afternoon I went swimming at the Mulholland Tennis Club. The teen-agers at that spot are an inspiration to those who believe in corporal punishment. There could not be a more whining, spoiled, lethargic group of children anywhere. But this afternoon, the pool was empty. I swam back and forth for about twenty minutes, staring up at the magnificent blue sky without a trace of clouds or smog. This, I thought, is Hollywood dreaming. I loved the slight breathlessness of prolonged swimming and the coolness of the water. It was heavenly until two teen-agers appeared and stared at me.

"What's he doing here?" one of them said.

"I don't know," the other one said. "Maybe his option didn't get picked up." They did not know me. I was just an adult in a pool. Neither of them was older than fourteen. One, a boy, jumped into the pool.

"Ick," he said to the girl. "The water's awful."

To me, it seemed like perfect water, cool and delightful.

"Ick," the boy said. "The water has too much chlorine. It's all smoggy, like the Valley."

"Ick," the girl said, screwing up her mouth, "the Valley."

March 1, 1977

There are devil-worshipers up here in the hills near my new house, people say. I do not know. I do know that there are many houses set on bluffs behind enormous gates, at the end of long, winding driveways, shielded from view. As I walk my dog past the gates, I see signs saying: BE-WARE—TRAINED ATTACK DOGS or NO TRESPASSING—YOU ARE WARNED.

I have often imagined strange rituals involving human sacrifice and sexual orgies behind those gates. I see, in my mind's eye, black-robed men and women trooping about an altar of silver bearing a pentagram. By day those people are accountants and dentists and grocery clerks, but by night their hands turn to the devil's work. So I imagine.

This morning there may have been some evidence. For about a week an enormous mobile home had been parked on Mulholland Drive, just forty or fifty feet from my house. Someone set it on fire this morning and tried to push it over the cliff onto a house below. "A fire bomb," the police officer told me. "Probably some kids," he said.

Diane, my neighbor, told me that she might have been able to predict it. She had slept with violent dreams all through the night, she said. She had dreamt of blood and screaming. "Probably that pizza," I said. It was a joke.

She looked at me with her gray eyes. "Are you crazy?" she asked. "The devil had communion with me last night."

Those were her words: "had communion with me." It makes me wonder what is going on in these hills and in my house. I will try to keep on Diane's good side.

March 3, 1977

Dinner tonight at the Mandarin with some friends. One woman started to bait me about Nixon, as she usually does. The time has long since passed when I will argue with her about it. Still, she continued to bait me. "I want him to die, Ben," she said. "I want him dead." That sounded extreme. Still, I did not argue with her.

Talk turned to the state of the world. Everyone at the table except me believes and knows as a certainty that a conspiracy of old Nazis and new conglomerates rules the world.

"The eight families," one man said knowingly. "The eight families."

When I told them they were dreaming, they looked at me as if I had exposed myself. "Just wait," they said. "Just wait."

They finished their meal with great gusto and then asked me how much the Rockefellers had paid me not to expose the conspiracy.

"Pass the mu-shu pork," I said. I don't have to worry about that crap any longer. I am in Hollywood now.

March 4, 1977

My superstitiousness grows apace. Yesterday I visited my agent at his house high in the hills of Trousdale. With him were two wheels from Warner.

"This kid has a great idea," my agent said. Then he turned to me. "Now tell it to them, and don't leave anything out."

I told them my idea for a book. They listened intently. One of them began to whisper to the agent while I spoke to the other about early California life.

"We don't want your exposure to be too large," the agent said. "So I'd like a hundred thousand up front against another four hundred thousand if the book comes out right."

I started to hyperventilate. I could only stop from giggling by biting my cheek.

Everyone was happy. My agent walked me to the door and said, "We'll get you a hundred grand up front, and that's just for starters. You could make a million dollars off this if you do it right."

As I drove down the hill, I felt like I was sailing. Where did I take my lucky turn? How could this all have turned out so wonderfully? I will have to be careful to make sure my luck does not change. Maybe I will see an astrologer.

I cannot think of anything I have done differently, and now people are talking about hundreds of thousands of dollars. What will I do with all that money? How can I make sure that my luck does not change?

March 6, 1977

Another episode of the velvet alley: I went to see a lawyer this morning about a small tax problem. He shook my hand, asked me all about myself, and then told me that to solve my problem, he had to know me "like a brother." He needed to know how much I had in the bank, how much property, how much stock, and so forth. His small ballpoint pen flashed in the light from the window as it flew across a pad of paper. I told him everything I could think of. He smiled at me and asked me if I could tell him how to become a writer.

"I'm sick of being a lawyer," he said.

I told him to write something and see how it turned out.

"All I do is these damned articles that no one pays me for," he said.

Then we talked about the tax problem. I had an idea it was covered by something I had read about in the *Wall Street Journal.*

The lawyer had never heard of it and seemed grateful to know about it. "That'll take care of it," he said.

"Just one more thing," he said as I walked out. "What was your name again?"

His secretary handed me a bill for two hundred dollars for the morning's work.

March 12, 1977

Dinner at the Palm last night with my friend with the blue-green eyes. On our way out, a wrinkled woman with a black dress and large warts and a reedy voice approached us. She held out a trembling hand and told us, "I have something to tell you. Something important."

With short, urgent breaths, she said to the girl with blue-green eyes, "I can read your face. You have had much trouble with men, especially one man in particular, a married man who says he loves you but will never be yours."

The girl with blue-green eyes stopped in her tracks and listened. Her grip tightened on my upper arm.

"You have let much money slip through your fingers in recent years—yes, in the last five years. You always need money."

The girl with blue-green eyes stared unabashedly.

"There is a woman who means to harm you. She will harm you if she can. She is jealous of you. She will hurt you. You must be helped."

The mouth of the girl with blue-green eyes dropped open.

"I can help you if you let me. I will light candles for you. I will say prayers for you. But the candles are expensive. I must have fourteen dollars immediately."

The girl with blue-green eyes looked at me and then at the woman, and said, "It sounds interesting. Have your agent call my business manager."

The girl with blue-green eyes has changed a lot. Six months ago she would have talked to the old woman about her soul and then given her money. Now she is thinking about what is going on right now. That is what counts. At least, that's what I tell her.

March 14, 1977

Frustration is a powerful drug. It can make people act irrationally. This afternoon my hustling friend Mike called and asked what I was doing. He said that he had just taken a drink of All Star Protein Supreme. "It gets metabolized or synthesized or something right away. It makes you high. It gives you a hard on for a week."

I asked him what he did this afternoon when he took it.

"I went out and killed some ants, man," he said. "I found their nest and poured poison all over their babies. When they came back, they really looked pissed."

That tells me a lot about life in Hollywood, but it does not apply to me. Not yet.

March 15, 1977

L.A., wonderful L.A. I got a call this morning from Janet, the hooker who wants to own a stockbrokerage firm. She wanted to have lunch with me. She offered to pay, which was nice.

At the Palm, she told me that she thought she now had enough money to buy a seat on the New York Stock Exchange and then set up an office in La Jolla, which is what she wants to do. How, she wonders, will she explain all the money to the IRS, should they come around? Would I pretend to be an investor in her brokerage? She would make it worth my while. In every way.

Janet looked lovely. She wore a sleeveless blue dress, darker than her eyes, but still wonderfully matching, and a thin gold bracelet. Her hair was long, but not in a disgusting Farrah Fawcett style. The food was great, as it always is at the Palm. People I knew came by, shook hands and looked enviously at Janet. I wondered if she had screwed any of them. It didn't matter. She was far from being my girl friend.

After lunch, we went for a ride up Benedict Canyon. On either side of the road, tall, arching palm trees soared into a light-blue sky. Cool air poured out of the air-conditioning vents. James Taylor sang over the stereo.

The sun reflected off the beige, slightly metallic hood of my car and highlights shone on the windshield. Janet sang along with the radio: "Sweet dreams. Flying machines. Pieces on the ground."

This is L.A. This is where everything comes together. This is where when you're there, you're all there.

I told Janet I would think about the offer.

March 17, 1977

Tonight, after I got home from seeing *Rocky* at a theater in the Valley where a girl with a face like an angel sold popcorn and orange crush, a figure emerged from the shadows around the carport, and scared me half to death. It was Sean, the drug dealer who operates out of his parents' basement. He looked scared.

"Can we talk?" he asked.

He was worried, he said, about the police closing in on him. "Either that or some very bad Mexicans," he said. He wanted to know if he could dig a hole in my backyard and stash some cocaine there until things were cool. "I'll lay some money on you," he said in a charmingly dated lingo. He did not look charming, though. He looked scared.

I told him that it was out of the question. I suggested that he rent a safe-deposit box at the bank and put the dope there. He said he would think about it.

"But," he said, "don't tell anyone about this. The code of the underworld, O.K.?" He said that and then he drove off back to his parents' basement.

March 19, 1977

Super day. My agent told me this morning that he has made a deal with a big paperback house for me to get two hundred thousand dollars for my book, which I have not even written yet. I hardly knew what to do. I pretended as if I had expected to get more, and in a way, I had. Still, that is real money.

I tried to figure out whether that was more than everyone in my office at the *Wall Street Journal* made put together. I think it almost is, but not quite.

How did it happen? How did my luck get so great? I asked Diane, my neighbor, if she had said any special prayers to the devil for me.

"He does not deal in money," she told me disdainfully.

Maybe he doesn't, but he's the only one. It is fantastic to think of that kind of money. It is almost enough to test whether it will buy happiness. I bought the girl with blue-green eyes dinner at the Mandarin to celebrate. We had both dumplings and soup to start with. That's what you can do with real money.

March 20, 1977

Suddenly I am in demand. I hinted, just hinted, to my friend Tony about how much I would get for my book. He told everyone we both know. My telephone has not stopped ringing. Another young hustler, Lenny, called, seething with envy. He could barely control his rage. Even over the telephone, I have an idea of his mouth, with the lips pulled back, baring his teeth.

I can understand it. That is how I once felt about other people making it. Let the rest worry about me now.

That is a childish attitude, but it is far from unusual. I must try to figure out what made my luck so wonderful and keep doing it.

Perhaps my dog brings me luck. I will have to be even kinder to her. Perhaps I will get her her own room.

Both Mary the person and the girl with blue-green eyes say that I am obsessed with that dog. The problem is that if I don't believe the dog brought me luck, I won't know where it came from. The dog is always here.

March 21, 1977

Dinner last night with the girl with blue-green eyes and A., former teammate on the *Wall Street Journal* editorial page. He appeared at the Mandarin, hair neatly combed, unobtrusive business suit in place. He and I talked about the news and politics, although I do not care about politics much anymore.

He did not like L.A., he told me. He did not care for the smog or the freeways or the way people dressed. He told me a story. Fifty years ago, a hunchback from the East visited Los Angeles. The hunchback had always been spurned and mocked in the East. When he visited Chinatown in Los Angeles, he found that the Chinese were extremely deferential. They virtually worshiped him. The hunchback found out the Chinese revered hunchbacks, considering that deformity to be a sign of heavenly blessing. So the hunchback simply stayed in Los Angeles's Chinatown forever.

A. leaned back in his chair, took off his wire-rimmed glasses and rubbed them with great care, well satisfied with his story.

"We should have warned you about that dumpling you're eating," the girl with blue-green eyes said. "If you aren't used to them, they can keep you up all night."

I wanted to kiss her, right there at the restaurant.

March 22, 1977

A black and ashen day. All my deals have fallen through. While I talked to a producer at the studio this afternoon, I picked up the telephone and called my agent in New York. I wanted to find out what was happening about my huge deal. Yesterday I had heard that a major hard-cover publisher was interested too.

In a cracking and raspy voice, my agent said that he had some disappointing news for me. "———, the paper-back fellow, decided he didn't want the book. I don't know why. So that's out."

I felt as if I were drowning. "What about———, the hard-cover people?" I asked.

"They're out too," he said. "They want to wait until they see how your first book does."

"What the hell do I do?" I asked.

"I don't know, boychik," he said. "We'll have to think about it."

I hung up the telephone. The whole world was collapsing around me. I could see the cars speeding by on Sunset Boulevard, but I felt as if I were not part of the world. I do not think I have ever felt such keen disappointment—not in love, not in health, not in anything.

I told the producer in the office what had happened.

"That's agents," he said. "They're always screwing things up."

I was too shaken to sit in the control booth during the taping that afternoon of the show I work on. I smoked one cigarette after another. I started to hope that I had cancer, that I would get cancer. I just wanted to evaporate.

After a few hours, I felt better. But Jesus, what will I

do? The whole thing is predicated on fast forward motion. When that stops, what do I do?

I sat in my living room tonight trying to figure out what had made my luck change. I would give anything to know. How on earth will I sleep tonight?

March 23, 1977

The girl with blue-green eyes, who really is a super friend, tried to help me understand why I am so shaken about the deals falling through. "Maybe it has to do with your mother pushing you, or maybe with competing with your father."

Her thoughts pass the time, but they are not really interesting. Suppose I found out that I was trying to succeed for a reason based upon childhood experiences. Would that make me want to do less? Would I trade in my Mercedes on a Honda? I do not think so. Anyway, I am like the confirmed junkie. I do not want to stop writing and hustling. I want to do well, not hear about why I should be content with doing less well. No one is interested in a bum's explanations, I told the girl with blue-green eyes. Least of all, the bum.

She looked at me sorrowfully and told me that I was not a bum. That is what friends are for, but what I want is another deal. I want to write, not hear theories.

March 24, 1977

Blessed relief. My agent had got things confused. The hard-cover people were indeed interested and wanted to talk in New York. The people at ———, another big paperback house, are interested too. Somehow the agent did not get that information through.

L.A., people say, is a human stock market. But stocks have no pain and I had plenty. I had enough in the last two days to kill a Russian infantry division.

Still, there are some lessons. Nothing can ever mean so much to me again that I will wish I had cancer because of losing it. And if that is L.A. life, L.A. life is fucked up.

This is the most distressing part. I felt so bad that not even L.A. made me feel better.

March 27, 1977

I am still shaken about the whole business of the deals falling through. Why did it happen? I tried to think whether anyone might have laid a curse on me. Only Diane, my neighbor, claims to have anything to do with the devil, and she is indignant at the mere hint that she might have laid a curse on me.

"I told you," she sniffed, "that Lucifer is not interested in your petty money matters." It's writing too, and not just money, but I didn't argue with her.

My friend Sean had a good idea. "Go back to the desert," he said. "You just might need to get your aura balanced."

It sounded right to me, although I have no idea what it means. Sometimes things are like that. They sound right, without my knowing what they mean. What does the "SLC" in Mercedes 450 SLC stand for? What does the "450" stand for? Who knows? And yet they sound right.

So off I went, by myself into the desert, about noon. There was almost no traffic on the San Bernardino Freeway. My wonderful car bore me along without a sound, farther and farther from the city. I turned on my stereo and listened to the rock-'n'-roll. I almost never listen to the news for more than a few minutes at a time. I have seen the news made, up close; I have learned that it is bunk. I am not interested in where Jimmy Carter went or what he had to say. It signifies nothing to me. He is running his promotion and I am running mine. If there were some real news, I would listen. But I have begun to understand why people here read only *Variety* and the *Hollywood Reporter*. They know, these smart people, what news is, and they know what part of it applies to them. That part is in the *Hollywood Reporter* and *Variety*. The headlines in the L.A. *Times* are only for time-wasting. They are not for people who are busy with their own lives.

So off I went, pulling into an almost deserted Palm Springs. There were still old people on the sidewalks, eating fudge from white bags, but no traffic jams. I swept through town without stopping and went to my hotel. In a few minutes I lay out in the burning sun, feeling how good it was after the gray morning in L.A. The healing, annealing sun. And yet this, too, is L.A. You can even see the L.A. smog from the mountains around Palm Springs. Here, in sunny Southern Cal, the sunshine is only a short drive away. Blessed be the sun. Around me, old people with New York accents talked about their children, every one of whom was a doctor and a lawyer and a millionaire manufacturer and a scholar and a lovable rascal.

At night, the town was eerily empty. I walked by the fudge place. It was closed. Back at the hotel, after a wonderful meal, I got a call from my agent. I had a firm offer from a reputable producer to buy an option on my book. Incredible! Perhaps my aura really had changed. I made a note to get a house in the desert as soon as possible.

I slept in an immense bed, next to open windows giving on a little patio. Moonlight poured into the room. The wind whipped the white linen curtains up against my face. In the distance I could hear people laughing and a piano playing. The desert was a tangible presence inside my room. I loved its warmth and its cleanliness. I feel as if it has cleansed me of my anguish about those goddamn deals.

Two much time making deals. Not enough time writing. That is what the desert said.

April 2, 1977

My friend, Danny the coke dealer, is in the hospital. I do not know how he got there. I know that he had to go in an ambulance last night, but I do not know why. His parents are at the hospital, Santa Monica, and he is not allowed to have any other visitors. I have no idea of whether it was related to drugs or not. I hope not. I hope it was not gunshot wounds. Not all drug dealers operate out of their parents' basement.

April 5, 1977

Debi, my friend who is a proselytizing Orthodox Jew, a physicist and a crank, called me this morning.

"You should see me," she said. "I've just stopped eating." She told me that she'd had a torrid romance since I last saw her.

"O.K.," I said.

"I look great," she said. "Can I come over to see you?"

"Of course," I said.

A few hours later, she pulled up in a Jaguar XK-E, convertible top down. At first I did not recognize her. She had bleached her hair blond. She wore it in a Farrah Fawcett. Her fingernails were painted silver. I thought I might cry.

"Don't I look Hollywood already?" she asked.

"I'm not sure," I said.

"Well, excuse me for breathing," she said.

I hope she moves back to New York very soon.

April 6, 1977

I saw Danny in the hospital this afternoon. He looks weak, but cheerful. As it happened, his problem was not gunshot wounds at all, but rather a severe virus which he had apparently gotten because he is so underweight and never eats. The reason he never eats is that he is always so coked up that he is not hungry. I wonder if there is an element of attempted chic in there too.

Anyway, Danny lay on his hospital bed with a pinkish translucent-plastic tube going into his arm, just below the elbow. "I'd like to put some coke into that tube," he said. "Wow, what a rush."

I think that is not exactly the conclusion he is supposed to draw from his misfortune. It worried me. "Aren't you a little scared about the drug situation?" I asked him.

"Why should I worry?" he asked. "There are plenty of drugs around. I won't run out."

Outside, I ran into Danny's father, a serious-looking, bearded surgeon. We talked for a minute. "After this," he said, "I'm going to make sure that Danny goes to law school."

April 7, 1977

Lisa M. and I had lunch together today. She is one of my former students from college-teaching days. Now she works as a secretary at an antique car dealership, which is frankly more than my course prepared her for. I showed her how to watch movies intelligently, which seemed more important to everyone at the time than it does now.

Lisa is probably the prettiest girl I know in L.A. She has icy, beautiful blue eyes and absolutely perfect, dainty facial features. But she has been troubled about what direction her life should take. I advised her to go into real estate brokerage. Everyone makes money at it, so they say.

"I think I've finally found myself," she said at lunch today. She had spent Sunday on a yacht off Newport Beach with a wealthy record company executive and his two mistresses, all having group sex. "I think I could really be awfully good at that," she said. "Everybody told me I was the hit of the party. Richard [the host] wants to take me to meet all his friends. He says I could be somebody to look up to." Richard told her that while she was going down on his black mistress his white mistress "did" him. So she says.

"Richard took pictures," she said. She showed me the pictures while the waiters chattered in Chinese behind me. I do not know if they could see. The pictures were good evidence that her story was true.

"I think," she said, "that this really solves a lot of my problems about what I could do. I mean, I could just have Richard take me to parties for the next ten years, or at least until my looks go. How long do you think that will be?" Lisa is twenty-four and I told her she had a lot of good years left. If you can call them good years.

"I think," Lisa said as she got her fortune cookies, "that I have finally started living up to my full potential as a human being."

April 9, 1977

Mike, my hustling friend, came over to lunch today. We went down to a vegetarian restaurant. I hate vegetarian food, but I love the girls who hang out there, skinny, with straight backs and wonderful legs. They can probably tell by my aura that I am a meat eater, so they stay away from me. But I like to look.

Mike told me, as he has told me for the last few months, that he is at the end of his rope. "I'm dying here, man," he said. "I'm just going fucking crazy, you know?"

I did not know exactly, but I nodded.

"My wife's driving me crazy. I feel like executing her," he said.

I chewed on a roll, which is about the only vegetarian dish I can stand.

"Sometimes I think I'll just cash out and go to another town, without my wife, if you know what I mean."

"What other town might you go to?" I asked.

"I don't know, man," he said. "But I feel like I've got to get out." He looked extremely unhappy.

He told me about an idea he had for a movie about a whole town that had taken LSD. "It could be a classic," he said. "A real epic." He waved his cream cheese sandwich in the air. "That's what I'll do. I'll make that movie." He looked happy.

Mike sells stationery and can barely afford to pay for his Toyota, but I did not want him to execute his wife, so I said, "It sounds good to me."

"It's art," he said, "you know?"

"Really," I said. "Could be very commercial."

He patted his stomach with satisfaction. "A real classic," he said, and I tuned out. It's better to just watch the girls.

April 17, 1977

Roxanne has surfaced. I had not heard from her since I moved into my new house, and now she is back on the scene. She has just been fired from her new job, the one she used to not go to and leave early and get stoned at, because she was so good at what she did that she was a threat to her superiors. She wants to go back to her parents in Oregon for a while, "for a little R & R," as she says. As far as I can tell, R & R is all she ever does.

She came up to my house and made oohing and ahhing sounds. She had a proposition to make. If I would let her live in my guest bedroom, she would "take care" of me. Right there on my porch, with the pine trees swaying gently in the breeze, she showed me that there is still pride of work in the United States of America. I was tempted to take her up on her offer and request, until she told me that she also wanted to borrow eight hundred dollars from me. She told me that at a particularly bizarre time. I wonder where she learned to do that.

So I had to turn her down. Now, she says, she has no choice but to go off to her parents, deep in the north country. I shall miss her.

April 21, 1977

As I walked by Hunter's Book Store yesterday, I saw a bedraggled black man carrying a picket sign. The sign said that Hunter's was unfair to black authors, would not carry their books, and would not understand the black experience in America.

The picketer spied me and noticed that I was reading the sign. It was a most unusual sight in Beverly Hills. The police would surely be there in a moment.

"Hey, man," he asked, "you want my book?"

Before I could escape, he showed me a hand-lettered book jacket attached to a sheaf of paper. The book's title was "How to Be a Successful You."

The picketer held out a grimy hand. "It's only $9.95," he said. "Buy one and intensify the class struggle."

April 22, 1977

A postcard came yesterday from my former student Isaiah.
He is a young black man of twenty-four whose most distin-
guished act so far was wearing a red velvet dress to his
high school graduation. He is not gay. He likes to shock
people. When he was told he could not get his diploma
if he wore a dress, he changed to a tuxedo, but still wore
full woman's makeup on his face.

He never graduated from college. He has not held a
job since he was born. About a year ago, he married a
beautiful girl who adores him. They lived on handouts
from their parents in a one-bedroom apartment in West-
wood that makes a pigsty look like the operations room
at the State Department.

Then last February, they moved to Mexico City, for
no apparent reason. Isaiah's wife works as a topless go-
go dancer while Isaiah stays home and watches TV game
shows.

The postcard said: "I think I'm onto something about
how America lives. It could be worth a lot of money. Are
you interested?"

Sometimes I wonder if Isaiah is responsible.

April 26, 1977

Fortunes can change suddenly in Hollywood. Today at lunch I had a visit from Rhonda, my hard-luck friend who wanted to have babies for hire. She is barely alive and looked it. I hope she does not fade out while she's visiting me. We sat on my deck eating leftover chicken, Shake 'n Bake Barbecue Style, my favorite food. Mike, my hustling friend, dropped by unannounced. He was jubilant. He has made it, or so he says.

Last week he met a guy, "a real loser with dandruff and everything," who had invented a device that makes guitar riffs sound like they are being played on your spine. "I took this schmuck straight to my lawyer," Mike said, "and I gave him five thousand dollars for the rights to the whole goddamn thing. I didn't even give him cash. Just a note and a thousand dollars." For that, Mike got the riff device. He took it, in the back seat of his Toyota, to a recording studio and showed it to them. He is now leasing it to them for one thousand dollars a week.

Rhonda looked so excited that I thought she would have a stroke. After Mike left, I asked Rhonda what had got her so jacked up.

"Are you crazy?" she asked. "That guy is going to be rich. He's not going to live in a one-room guesthouse with three dogs."

I told Rhonda he was married.

"So was Zsa Zsa," Rhonda said.

May 1, 1977

Dinner last night with Lisa M., my beautiful friend who thought she had "found herself" in group sex a few weeks ago. Yesterday, she was down in the dumps. I tried to comfort her, because I like her a lot. She's never done anything bad to me.

The weekend before, her rich friend Richard had called her at work and asked her, told her, to come over to his house in Marina Del Rey. "Don't eat anything after lunch," he told her.

When she got there, Richard and his particolored mistresses were there. So was a tall, hefty blond woman wearing a leather corset, high-heeled boots and net stockings. "Her name was Sheba," Lisa told me. "Richard told me I had to do everything she said. He told me not to appeal to him for anything because Sheba was in control." As before, Lisa had pictures that seemed to prove her story.

Lisa was stripped and allowed to sniff cocaine. Then she was bound hand and foot and a leather "discipline helmet" was put over her face and head. "They zipped the mouth shut, and that scared me," Lisa said. Then she was wrapped in a blanket and put in an empty bathtub. "It wasn't bad," Lisa said. "I started to fall asleep."

While Lisa told the story, hustling young men wearing thin leather jackets and gold chains kept drifting by our table at the Palm to catch a glimpse of Lisa. She is that pretty. Lisa did not touch the wonderful onions or her steak.

"Then Sheba dragged me out of that bathtub and chained my hands to a bedpost. She started to whip me with a big bullwhip. I tried to cry, but I couldn't because of the discipline helmet," she said, gingerly poking at her salad. I hoped that no one I knew was overhearing the conversation.

"Finally, they took off the discipline helmet and I could see Richard had one of the girls, the blond one, doing him. That's when I started to scream. I had blood all over my wrists from where they were tied up. Finally, Richard told Sheba to let me up." She took a forkful of fried onions. There were tears in her wonderful blue eyes just remembering it. "Afterwards, Richard sent me home in a taxi all the way back to North Hollywood, which is a long ride. But I have to wonder," she said.

"I'll say," I said.

"Really," she said.

"You know," she said, "Richard has never told me he loved me or liked me or anything." She looked pained. "I just have to wonder," she said, "if he's sincere."

May 3, 1977

When I go out of town overnight, I have Lester, a heavy-set man of about forty, sit for Mary the dog.

Lester came here from Indiana about ten years ago with a million dollars, or so he says. He wanted to be a producer. Since he did not know any better, he commissioned a few writers to write books for him. Then he tried to sell them to studios. They could see him coming, so they got him to put up money for production deals, development deals, every kind of deal.

No movies were made, and Lester is probably the only person in this town who is surprised.

Lester wanted to live the L.A. life, so he bought a Rolls-Royce convertible. "It cost me a thousand a month in repairs alone," he says.

Lester is a fund of stories of misadventure and suffering. Someone took his deposit on a house and would not return it. Someone else took his hand-made leather luggage. He sold his house just before the real estate boom started.

I like Lester a lot. He genuinely loves the dog. Ordinarily I try to stay away from unlucky people, but Lester is different. He is quite cheerful about his lot in life, and that makes him not a loser.

The girl with blue-green eyes likes Lester too. "He's very gallant," she says.

He had better be. He does not have a cent of that million left and now he is earning money baby-sitting dogs.

May 4, 1977

Isaiah and his lovely bride got back from Mexico City last week. Today they came over to visit me. Isaiah looked like he had been expelled from a motorcycle gang for looking too degenerate. His wife looked blond and waiflike, as usual.

I asked him what he was going to do now.

He shrugged his thin shoulders. "I don't know. I guess I'll run for Congress," he said. He was not joking. He plans to start his campaign in the fall. "It'll be great," he said. "I'll have all these brunches and everything. You can be an adviser."

His lovely wife looked at me brightly. "Can we count on you for a thousand dollars?" she asked sweetly.

May 5, 1977

A visit last night from Peter B., a former classmate at Yale and an intelligent guy. He listened to my stories about L.A. and said I had changed. "Who hasn't?" I asked.

"It's kind of an absurdist thing," he said. "I can't exactly pin it down, but it's like a shift from the logical to the absurd." He paused for a minute. "Not that I'm making a value judgment, of course," he said.

Of course. But he has a point. The logical point of view carried with it some idea of limits, of slow and orderly progress and decline. The Hollywood view, the absurdist view, says that anything can happen. That makes sense to me, although I begin to wonder what "sense" means in the city of the angels.

May 7, 1977

Lunch at the Palm today with my hustler friend Tony. He wanted to borrow money from me, but I shined it on. That hurt his feelings and he did not say anything for a while. Then he said, "See that guy over there? A few weeks ago, he didn't have a buck, and now he's raking it in." He pointed at a booth to my right. In the booth was Mike. He looked happy.

Next to Mike was Rhonda. She looked happy too. She was wearing a pair of bleached Levi's and a black T-shirt with white letters that said DONNA SUMMER. Across from them was a guy about my age with a heavy-set but muscular build. He wore a leather jacket. His eyes were puffy. Next to him was a thin blond girl with a whining look on her face. She wore a gray jumpsuit with American flag patches on the shoulders. She twirled a fried onion in her right hand.

I went over to say hello. "Ken," Mike said to his friend, "this is a guy you should know. Ben Stein. Ken Snyder. Ben and I used to talk about how to make it before I got the Riffmaster." He smiled broadly. "I think maybe Ben really just wanted to sit in a room and write," he said. "Ben introduced me to Rhonda," he said. Rhonda giggled.

Ken Snyder did not look up. It was just as well. Up close, he did not look like someone I wanted to know.

"You know Ken Snyder?" Tony asked. He was impressed until I told him I did not know Ken Snyder. "Ken Snyder is, as far as I'm concerned, Mr. LP—Mr. Long-Playing Record—in this town."

"Really," I said. The girl next to Ken Snyder still twirled her fried onion and looked bored.

May 10, 1977

A major, major screenwriter, the biggest, sat next to me at dinner a week ago. I had known him slightly before. We told each other funny stories. Suddenly, after I told a story about a gangster in England, he grabbed my arm. "That's it," he said. "That's the story I've been looking for." He fixed me with sincere, watery blue eyes, the kind of eyes a dog would have if he could have blue eyes. "Would you be interested in writing a script of that with me?" he asked. "Would you have the time?" His voice was almost pleading. It was the approximate equivalent of being asked by a certified saint if you wanted to have the cancer in your lungs cured.

"Of course," I said. "That would be great."

"When can you start?" he asked.

I mentioned a date four weeks away. He shook his head firmly.

"Not soon enough," he said.

"I'll start tomorrow, if you want," I said, breathless.

"That's my boy," he said. He put his arm around my shoulder and said to our hostess, a famous mogul's widow, "I love the way this guy's head works. I love it."

I went home in a cloud. For five days, I could not reach the famous writer on the telephone. Finally, I got him on the phone this afternoon.

"When can we start?" I asked him.

"Well," he said, "I've been thinking about that idea, and I think maybe some other people have already been there. Know what I mean? But I like the way your head works. I really do. Know what I mean?"

"Yes," I said. I felt as if someone had dropped the World Trade Center onto my abdomen.

"So I'm going to look for another property for us to work on. I like your head, Benjy," he said. Then he got off the phone.

Now I know why so many astronauts go crazy.

May 12, 1977

Lisa M. was feeling low this afternoon, so I took her to the Mandarin for dinner. She is lonely, she said. She stopped seeing Richard, the sadist, and now she has decided that all men are beasts. I wonder what she thinks I am.

She picked at her spring rolls and asked me if I thought she should take est. I do not know if Lisa would profit from it. I also do not like to give advice. People never appreciate it.

"I have to do something new," she said. "I have to change my life." She sat back as the waiter took away the appetizer and served her lemon chicken.

"Maybe I should shave my pubic hair," she said. "That might do it."

"Really," I said.

May 15, 1977

This evening, while I was reading *Captains and the Kings* as the girl with blue-green eyes read *Gone With the Wind,* the doorbell rang. Mary the dog went berserk, as she always does. At the door was Mike. He never travels with his wife anymore, and she was not there. Instead, he was with Rhonda, who wore a look of crazed glee. Behind them was a middle-aged blond woman with craggy features and piercing eyes, even in the dark.

Mike introduced Helga von Kreuznach as "my leader, my mentor in bioenergetic testing." That meant that she was a masseuse. In a heavy German accent she told me and the girl with blue-green eyes that she could "do groovy things with couples, depending on what comes up." Giggle, giggle.

Very subtle. I told Mike that I'd pass. The girl with blue-green eyes looked like she would murder everyone in the room. She is quite puritanical about things like that.

Rhonda looked up at us brightly. Her hair was much blonder than it had been. "Do you want to watch us?" she asked.

"Do you want me to shoot you?" the girl with blue-green eyes asked.

Helga said, "It is hard to make this work if you are fighting it."

"Fuck you, you Kraut cunt," the girl with blue-green eyes said.

After they left, the girl with blue-green eyes returned to her book. She read for about half an hour and then said, "You know who I like better than Scarlett? I like Mrs. O'Hara. She always knows how to act."

Later that night Mike called to tell me that he was sorry

161

he had got the girl with blue-green eyes so jacked up. "But it certainly doesn't mean that I can't be your friend, I hope," he said.

"Tell him to jerk off into a brown paper bag," the girl with blue-green eyes said, and returned to Tara.

May 16, 1977

Isaiah came over this afternoon to explain to me how his campaign would work.

"It's, like, groovy," he said. "Really, like, groovy. I'm gonna talk to all these, like, fat cats and, like, get them to, like, pay for everything."

"Sounds good to me," I said.

"We've, like, got to get the country right again, like, so that people can, like, slow down and, like, get calmed down."

"Really," I said.

"Like, I mean, enough is enough," he said.

"I can dig it," I said.

"It's, like, a bitchin' platform," he said.

"Why don't you send it in to the *New York Times* op-ed page?" the girl with blue-green eyes said.

May 17, 1977

We are casting every day, these days, for the right people to make jokes on a new comedy variety show on which I work. It's probably the most original show on TV. I drop in on the casting sessions and watch the actors and actresses lined up outside. They look nervous and scared. Their faces are oily and sweaty. Sometimes they have elaborate costumes or other tricks in boxes. They depress me. Often I see them, twenty years older than I am, pulling up in battered Plymouth Dusters and old Cadillacs. Is that the reward of Hollywood life? Why won't that happen to me? It scares me a lot. Will I wind up like that, begging crumbs at auditions? Of course, I am a writer and not an actor, but even so, it worries me. What have those people been doing all these years? Have they been going to tryouts now for year after year, time without end? Do they live in garden apartments with wavy green plastic railings along the balconies?

Almost none of the people who try out are going to get on the show. Their humor is too ethnic, too shticky, as they say. The show is supposed to take place in a small town in the Midwest, where there are no ethnics at all. That is explained to the auditioners. Nevertheless, we have people trying to be the local rabbi, the local Irish priest, the local Mafioso, the local Black Panther.

We have a woman trying to imitate Xavier Cugat's sex-bomb wife, Charo. She shakes her hips and rolls her eyes, but there are crow's feet around those eyes, and a lot of fat. The voice, supposed to be Cuban, is pure Brooklyn.

Another person comes in. He imitates a swami. It is not a bad gimmick until we hear his swami voice. Almost undiluted Yiddish. He looks hopeful and sweats under his fake turban. There is no way he will ever get on that show, but the casting director says, "Thank you. You were terrific."

It is always sad to see people thrusting themselves forward for something they have no chance of getting. It is a reminder to me to spend more time writing and less time making deals. I came to write, after all, not to wheel and deal. At least that's what I think I came for.

May 18, 1977

A heart-to-heart this afternoon with the girl with blue-green eyes. She has acted a little snappish with me and my friends lately. I hope, I told her, that she will tell me what is troubling her. After a great deal of hemming and hawing, she told me that she is upset because everyone else is getting ahead while she is out at the beach doing nothing.

I told her that she was under a severe delusion about that. "Hardly anyone gets ahead. If everyone got ahead, the ones who get ahead would not be so rare and so famous. And they wouldn't be paid so much."

She did not believe me. She told me the story of her family again, which I am getting to know intimately—the irresponsible mother, the remote father, the jealous brothers. I wonder what it all has to do with life in L.A.

"It applies," she said, "because if I can do something here, I won't need them or anybody else any more."

That, I told her, could not possibly be wronger. The adulation of a nation is not a substitute for a loving relationship with one person. That sounds like a cliché, but like so many clichés, it is true.

I told her that in her particular case, I was the person with whom she had that relationship.

That made her cry.

"You make me feel the worst of all," she said, "because you get so much done and yet you always are just lying in bed."

Funny thing. People have said that to me all my life. Why does anyone think that I am not getting something done just because I am lying in bed? Why does anyone assume that you have to be in torment to get anything done? Or standing up?

Still, I feel for the girl with blue-green eyes. Sometimes she looks like the young Elizabeth Taylor. I told her to shine it on and just keep writing. Then I took her to the Palm. As we stepped outside, a cool, dry breeze swept across the canyon, across Mulholland Drive, and blew across our faces. That is what it means to be in love in L.A.

"Don't force yourself to do anything," I told her. "It will come when it comes." She smiled a beautiful smile at me just as I realized I was beginning to sound like her.

May 24, 1977

At the Palm tonight a group of young white kids started to yell and scream. They hopped from table to table whooping and waving their arms. They did not come to my table, which was just as well. The girl with blue-green eyes wants to move to San Francisco, and we discussed it.

The people in San Francisco," she said, "are more my kinds of people. They aren't always in such a goddamned hurry."

"You have to decide," I told her, "whether you want to take it easy or get something done. Either one is a fine goal. Just decide which."

That started her crying, which she did not stop for the whole time it took me to eat my steak. I regretted having given advice. Many people do not appreciate it.

Later in the meal, she brightened up. "I guess I could go to San Francisco and get something done too, and that would show you."

No more advice. She said she would leave at the end of the week. There was nothing keeping her here, she said.

"I love you," I said.

"That's not important," she said. "Getting things done is important."

Off to the right, against a wall of drawings, I could see Mike with Rhonda. In front of Rhonda were both a steak and a lobster.

Across from Mike and Rhonda was Ken Snyder. He was by himself. He stared at Mike in a way that made me uncomfortable thirty feet away. Mike scowled and scratched his fork back and forth across the tablecloth.

Ken Snyder looked like a killer.

Rhonda took a bite from the lobster and then one from the steak. It was an awesome display of gluttony.

The girl with blue-green eyes said, "You'd probably like it if I went to San Francisco. You'd start up with Roxanne and those sluts again."

"Are you crazy?" I asked.

"That's not an answer," she said. She is getting quite smart.

I think she should go to law school, but not in San Francisco. I told her so.

"Don't patronize me," she said, and started to sniffle.

"I'm not patronizing you," I said, but things were pretty far gone.

Over at Mike's table, Rhonda was being served another dish of cottage fries. Ken Snyder was eying a live lobster. He looked like he would take it on with his teeth one on one. I hope Mike knows what he is doing.

I wish the girl with blue-green eyes would stay.

May 28, 1977

I cannot remember the last time it rained here. Perhaps
it was before I moved to L.A. Day after day there is not
a cloud in the sky. By noon, the chill of morning is gone
and a glaringly bright sun burns everything to a brownish-
tan color. The sun is too bright for the bare hills, and
they started some weeks ago to lose their appeal. Fires
are breaking out everywhere. Each day there are new ones
in canyons, in flatlands, everywhere. How do they get
put out? The sun fans them with its heat, and still, by a
miracle, they do not consume the entire city.

This afternoon, I went to see Leon, my producer friend.
He is a cocky little man who lives in that huge house in
Bel Air. On my way up the hill to see Leon, I was stopped
by a line of fire trucks. A clean-cut policeman wearing
dark glasses waved me away. "Brush fire," he said, and he
did not say any more. He did not need to say any more.
A fire in Bel Air, where $700,000 houses are lined up next
to each other, cheek by jowl. Once a fire started to really
move, it would be deadly serious, even if the houses were
hideous. In L.A., a hideous house often costs more than
a pretty one. Supply and demand.

I took an alternate route up to Leon's house. For some
reason, that route passed right by the fire area. Pumpers
were lined up along the side of the street and firemen
shot jets of water down into a canyon about six tenths
of a mile from Leon's house. It did not look serious.

Leon is restless. He can barely sit in the same seat for
more than thirty seconds. I understand that perfectly. In
his study are hundreds of pictures of famous people whom
I do not recognize. All the faces in the picture frames,

though, have the look of fame and confidence that makes me think I should know them.

"Who are all these people?" I asked Leon.

"I'll tell you later," he said.

I told him an idea for a book. He looked doubtful. "I think Universal is already going to make a bid," I said.

"Great idea," he said. "I'll pitch it to Universal."

He told me that he was going to Europe for six weeks. He will spend most of the time in Cadiz. "I'm taking Italian lessons," he said. "It's important to know the language."

We talked for a while longer. He told me I was a great kid. "I love you, Ben," he said. "I'm going to make a big sale on this book."

As I drove down the hill, the pumpers were already gone. A few firemen stayed behind to clean up. Other than that, there was no sign of a fire.

I thought about Leon and his Italian lessons. I wonder if he knows that Cadiz is in Spain.

May 29, 1977

I took the girl with blue-green eyes to the airport this afternoon. She is heading up to San Francisco. She did not want to take her car.

"It's just a material encumbrance," she said, "a reminder of L.A."

"It's good to have a car," I said, as well I knew.

"In San Francisco, you can walk," she said.

"You get places faster if you drive," I said.

"Only if you want to," she said, and she was right.

I am supposed to go see her in two weeks. I don't know if I can wait that long. On the way home from the airport, I cried for the first time since I moved to L.A.

Later, I drove over to the studio. On Sunset Boulevard, right in front of the studio, a middle-aged man with a short silver beard took money from his pocket and tore it up. He threw the shreds at passing drivers.

Instead of doing that, he might have gone to San Francisco.

June 2, 1977

The girl with blue-green eyes called tonight. She loves San Francisco. "You can breathe the air," she said. She is staying at a friend's apartment in Sausalito until she finds her own apartment in San Francisco.

"I've already written ten pages of my book," she said.

"I miss you," I said.

"That's not important," she said. "Getting things done is important."

After she hung up, I sat in the living room and looked at the lights in the Valley. I can see Barham Boulevard and Lankershim Boulevard stretching for miles. At Vanowen, there is a large intersection. The lights, tinted slightly green, form an immense cross. I wondered if the people at that intersection could see me.

The telephone rang again. The girl with blue-green eyes asked me to send her some money, just until she gets some out of her savings account. I told her I would.

Sometimes when people ask for money it is an assault. Sometimes it is a caress. This was a caress, of a strange kind.

June 12, 1977

We need a love interest for the show I am working on. She had to be blond and beautiful. I sat in the office of the creative supervisor while beautiful blondes traipsed in and out. Most of them had little talent and were not even truly beautiful up close. One of them was. She read her lines and then looked at me expectantly.

I did not know exactly what to ask her. "Have you had any experience appearing before a live audience?" I asked.

"Yes," she answered. "I was Miss America two years ago."

She looked at me with a hopeful, pleading look. I could hardly believe it. In high school the cheerleaders would usually ignore me.

After she left the office, I told the producer how great I thought she looked.

"Tell her that she has to get your personal approval before she gets the part," he said with a wink. I could not tell if he was serious. I talked to the former Miss America for a few minutes. She wanted the job so she could send her husband to medical school. I told the creative supervisor that someone else could make the decision. I already had my thrill.

June 14, 1977

There is a story making the rounds here about a junior agent who read a movie script. "It stinks," he told his boss. "It's crap."

"You're supposed to sell it, not smell it," his boss said.

I used to laugh at that agent, but I have an idea of what he is talking about. Yesterday we taped two particularly awful episodes of the show I work on.

"This was terrible," I said. "It just doesn't strike the right note at all," I told my boss.

In a cold and angry voice, my boss told me that I was not there to criticize. "If you don't like it," he said, "just put it in your memoirs. I don't want to hear about it unless you love it."

At first I was hurt by that, but then I thought there might be something to it. My job has no clear description. If they want me to never criticize, it is their money, and they can spend it as they see fit. No one forced me to take the job. But it does make writing alone in my little office on top of the mountain seem a lot better. I will get started on my memoirs soon. I went through the cult of personality once, and it was not that much fun in the end. There are plenty of people around who can get into cults. They do not need me.

June 15, 1977

I spend most of every afternoon, every beautiful Southern California afternoon, in a subterranean control booth for a TV studio. Above us, on the stage, a TV variety show is being taped. This afternoon, the control booth was filled with people. At a gleaming console covered with literally thousands of buttons-and levers, in front of a bank of fifteen TV monitors, sat the director, the assistant director, the production assistant, the assistant production assistant, the audio man, the tapes man and a stranger. All worked feverishly at their posts.

Behind them, in tall director's chairs, sat the creative supervisor, a major gun in TV production, the producer, the assistant producer, the creative vice-president, two creative consultants and someone's wife. All of us were being paid, and handsomely, to sit in that room and fervently watch the monitors for anything that might be improved.

On the monitors, a teen-age girl appeared in a bathing suit, holding a chicken in her arms. She sang "Goodnight, Irene" to the chicken. It was not funny. It was not sweet. It was boring. The creative supervisor started to sputter with rage. "Where in hell is her chicken suit?" he asked. "How the hell can this be good if she doesn't have on a chicken suit?"

Everyone sat forward and listened. The director looked frightened.

"Christ, I don't know," he said. "I never heard anything about a chicken suit."

The assistant producer tried to appear calm. "I never saw that girl in a chicken suit," she said.

Apologies and disclaimers went around the room. The creative supervisor stared at the director and said calmly,

"I do not see how we can make good television without a chicken suit. Do you?"

No one laughed.

The producer said that he would get the girl her chicken suit and tape her later. The creative supervisor leaned over to me and whispered in my ear. "It probably won't work with the chicken suit either. What do you think?"

"It doesn't work for me," I said. "But what the hell, let's try the chicken suit."

"Are you just saying that, or do you believe in the chicken suit concept?" he asked, still whispering.

"It's worth a try," I said.

"All right," the creative supervisor said in a louder voice. "We'll lose the act for now, but Jesus, I can't get over that chicken suit."

"Really," I said. "For sure."

June 16, 1977

This morning Lenny called to invite me to have lunch with him at the Palm. Lenny is a superhustler. He was in the garment business in New Jersey, but as he says, "I figured, 'Hey, man, it's all a scam, so why not go where it's warm?' " So here he is, trying to produce movies. Al says that a producer is one step away from a derelict, but that's not Lenny. Lenny always has deals just waiting to happen. He knows Julie and Warren and Goldie and everybody. Someday soon he's going to put me in his black Porsche and take me to meet all those people. But this morning, he wanted to meet me at the Palm at lunchtime. I said I would be there.

Lenny's friend and mine, Tony, was there. I met Tony a while ago. Tony is another hustler. He used to be an organizer for the grape strike, but he got wise too, just like Lenny. Tony figured that if he could organize poor *braceros*, he could do anything, and besides, he was tired of being poor. So there they both were, in their leather jackets, waiting for me at the Palm.

They were both in terrific humor. Terrific. "I think Metro is going to buy the ambulance story," Tony said. "Could be very doable."

"I'm hip," I said.

"We're looking for $250,000 in production fees alone," Lenny said with a wink. "That's not counting the percent of the net."

"Could be gross," Tony said. "We're going for gross, but it'll probably be net."

They were falling off their chairs with joy. "If Metro picks up the ambulance story, I think we'll be in great shape on the fisherman story," Lenny says. "It won't be long now."

"We'll be looking at gross deals only," Tony says, "after the fisherman deal."

They took out a piece of grimy notebook paper and started madly writing figures on it. Every few seconds they giggled. "Do you know anything about tax shelters?" Tony asked, his face suddenly serious. "We're sure as hell gonna need one after the fisherman deal," he said.

They became even more jocular. They started shouting across the room to friends. People stared at them. They didn't care. They were rich. They even let the wonderful onions get cold while they figured some more. They were going to be big-time producers. Very big.

"You know what Jack Warner said about the talent, Ben?" Tony asked.

"No," I said. I did know that I, as a writer, was considered "talent" and they, as "producers" were considered "money men."

"Talent is scum," Tony said. "That's what Jack Warner said. But you're special. We'll take care of you."

"You know what Harry Cohn said about writers, Ben?" Lenny asked.

I could imagine.

"Hacks with Underwoods. A dime a dozen," Lenny said. "That's what he said."

They started to go into a long discussion of where to live and what kinds of cars to get. "The Corniche convertible is nice," Tony said, "but a lot of niggers have 'em." He was talking about a $100,000 car. "I could stand a Jensen," Lenny said. That settled that. It was a Jensen for both of them. They would live in Bel Air, and have beach houses at the Malibu Beach Colony. Even the people at the next table started to pay attention.

The check came. Neither of them had any money. Lenny offered to pay me back the next week. Tony said it would have to wait until after the fisherman deal goes through. "But then," he said, "I'll buy you dinner at Perino's."

I am going to save the American Express receipt in a Lucite box to remind myself of what a hustler is and what I am.

June 17, 1977

Before I got out of bed this morning, I called the girl
with the blue-green eyes and asked her to come back. Her
writing is going poorly. She pooh-poohed me for a few
minutes and then she started to cry.

"I can't come back," she said, "until I've done something.
I can't live in L.A. and not do anything."

"You're my angel," I said, "and that's something."

"It's not enough for you," she said.

"Of course it is," I said. "It absolutely is."

She started to cry. "When will I ever get anything done?"
she asked.

"It only matters if you want it to matter," I said. "Not
otherwise. If I could rest, I would. I can't and so I work."
That's not quite true, but close enough.

I picked up the girl with the blue-green eyes at the Bur-
bank airport. As I drove us along Hollywood Way, past
the neat bungalows and the small shopping centers, I told
her I was glad she was back.

"Instead of my teaching you to do things, why don't
you teach me how to not do things?" I said.

"Really," she said, and started to sniffle.

June 20, 1977

Last night I went to see Joan Baez sing at the Universal Amphitheater. An explanation of a few terms. I said "see" instead of "hear" because she sounds so much better on records than live that the only reason to go is to see her famous face, floating above a purple cotton sari, an orange flower on one side of her black-and-gray hair, a white flower on the other side. "Sing" means a few songs delivered in Joan's wonderful voice in between long stretches of guitar tuning and imitations of Jewish accents. The Universal Amphitheater is an immense sunken outdoor dish, adjacent to an enormous parking lot, adjacent to the Hollywood Freeway. On the other side of the amphitheater is the Universal Tour.

As the legions of Joan Baez fans, bearded and almost hip, came riding in astride their BMWs, hundreds upon hundreds of BMWs, more BMWs in that one parking lot than in Bavaria, the Middle Americans, overweight and angry-looking in their faded leisure suits and frumpy dresses, blond, sullen kids in tow, left the tour area—where they had just seen the real shark from *Jaws*, actors falling off rooftops, and other thrills—in their Buicks and Winnebagos. The people in the BMWs looked slightly discomfited at seeing their historical and social parents staring at them, but they just turned up the stereo in their 2002s and shined it on. What does a person in a BMW, the car of those almost too hip to be concerned with material goods, have to say to a family in a Winnebago? Really.

People were passing around joints, furtively sneaking hits of coke out of master blasters, and generally grooving to the memories. It was an old crowd, my age or older, which means mid thirties, and hey, how cool is that?

No crazed-looking young people here, but instead, a lot of us old folks nodding as the familiar words flew past, toking up and whispering, "Really." Joan even made fun of us a little by comparing L.A. with Utah, but it was all mellow.

She sang about how she was not going to get turned around by nuclear power plants (scattered applause), the Trident submarine (bewildered silence), the neutron bomb (more applause) or Anita Bryant (wild applause). She sang about her beautiful childhood, about how fucked up Amerika still is, about how rock-'n'-roll stinks, and she imitated Jewish accents some more. The applause was generally good, but far from tumultuous.

At the intermission, a fat former student of mine appeared, her hair in braids. "You know," she said, "I wish Joan would concentrate more on nuclear power, because that's what's going to kill us all."

"Really," I said.

"I mean, we've got to fight Anita, for sure, but there'll always be gay people. We've got to worry about the San Onofre plant and everything. That nuclear power is bad stuff."

"Really," I said. "I can dig it."

Joan sang more songs, said a few four-letter words, and then belittled and exploited her relationship of long ago with Bob Dylan, who is to Joan Baez as the United States is to Guatemala. One of her manager's flunkies sat near me. Someone asked him why he had taken Joan to Columbia, away from A & M Records. "I thought Joan loved Herb Alpert," the questioner said.

"Joan needed more bread," the flunkie said. "It's as simple as that."

Onstage, Joan sang about how she would not let Amerika's greed turn her around.

After the concert, I stood in line at the exit behind two

men with beards and mirrored glasses (at 10:30 P.M.).

"Hey, what've you been doing?" the first one asked. "You still working in child care?"

"No, but it's cool," the second one said. "I'm at Rockwell."

Backstage, a Joan Baez accolyte whispered to me that her manager was in big trouble.

"Why?" I asked.

"The phones have stopped ringing," he said, looking conspiratorial in mirrored dark glasses and a T-shirt that said FUNKY KINGS.

"If you know what I mean."

I have no idea what he means.

June 22, 1977

Last night I went to a party given by a well-known writer. It was in honor of Stella Adler, a famous acting teacher. She sat in a lawn chair, swathed in a brown dress and jewelry, while directors, writers and producers wandered in and listened to a few pearls drop from her lips. "To be an actor is to be everything, to feel everything, to do everything," she said with an English accent, sweeping her hand grandly toward the Ventura Freeway. Then she told a story about some relation, perhaps a cousin, a lawyer, and, how he gets women such fabulous divorce settlements.

I sat next to a man whose wife had just died. He was now "dating" a dropped-out transsexual. "I like nuns," he said. "They're aggressive. They know how to get things done." He looked around furtively and then added, "They'll try anything too, if you know what I mean."

Later, I asked a middle-aged woman what she did. "What do I do, darling?" she asked. "What do I do?" She looked at me in a puzzled way. "I wake up. I listen to the birds. I walk in the fields. I live. I love. I am happy." She did not look happy, but still I said, "Really. Sounds great to me."

She looked at me for a moment. "It does?" she said.

June 27, 1977

Today is the official publication date of my first novel. I do not see any sign of a celebration from anyone. This afternoon I spoke at length to one of the producers at the studio about the book. I was disappointed, I said, that the publisher was not behind it more actively.

He had an idea. "You know, what would make a great book," he said, "is a book on edible pages. They could be chocolate-flavored or something like that, and then people could take them on trips and eat them as they read them. Most books aren't worth reading twice anyway," he said.

I will have to speak to my publisher about that.

July 6, 1977

Last weekend the studio I work for had a wonderful July Fourth picnic. It was like no other picnic I have ever seen. On a huge grassy spot, many tables had been placed, covered with checked cloths and laden with hot food. A band played. The food was excellent. People were smiling and happy. I liked it too. I saw two blond girls, dressed like flappers, with the son of a producer. They were cute as can be. I walked over to them and introduced myself. They were twenty-year-old twins who had just moved out from Indianapolis, or "India-no-place," as they said. They wanted to be stars.

They had already been picked up on the street by several famous men who wanted them to pose nude for various things before casting them in the parts that would make their careers. It was hard to tell if they had agreed. What was certain was that they were thoroughly on the make. I thought of all that could be done with two twenty-year-old blond twins from Indianapolis, and my head spun.

I do not know what stopped me from asking them both to the Palm for dinner. I guess I am slowing down. Now I cannot remember their names.

July 10, 1977

I love my house, but it is not a Spanish-style house, which is, I think, what I want. A Spanish-style house is more the stuff of dreams come true, although a little mountain aerie like mine is all right, too.

I have seen quite a few of them, and some of them are magnificent. Those are the ones that are too expensive. I have also seen a few that are beautiful but small. Those are also too expensive.

I am like the famous comedian. I do not want any house I can afford.

July 21, 1977

Before each taping of the variety show I work on, I watch the producer of the show appear before the live audience. The audience is mostly older people who have been brought in from communities for the elderly in Orange County. They stand outside in a broiling sun for about an hour and then are led into the studio, sound stage 4. They sit restlessly until the producer appears and tells a few jokes.

Just before the acting starts, the producer tells the audience that we, the studio, need tape of them clapping wildly. He says, "One, two, three, clap," and the audience claps wildly. Then the producer tells them that we need live laughter so that we won't need "sweetening" later. We will just use this very audience's laughter, taped before the show, and that makes all the difference.

No one in the audience ever catches on. At least, they say nothing. Instead, after "One, two, three, laugh," the audience laughs hysterically, slapping their sides, doubling over, tears rolling down their cheeks, wheezing for lack of breath.

The producer thanks them, then points out that there is nothing to laugh about and makes fun of them for laughing. It all fits in.

July 23, 1977

At the studio, two producers, Bobby and Jimmy, and I kicked around ideas of actors and actresses for a forthcoming pilot. I did not say much because I know so few actors. First we discussed the part of the father.

"How about R.C.?" Bobby asked.

"R.C.?" Jimmy said. "R.C. would be great. I love him."

"Oh, I love him too," Bobby said.

What about the secretary-adviser?

"How about F.F.?" Bobby asked.

"F.F. would be great," Jimmy said. "I love her. She's great."

"Absolutely," Bobby said. "I love her too."

The son?

"I love V.T.," Jimmy said.

"V.T. is terrific," Bobby said. "Can we get him?" He shook his head. "Jeez, V.T. would be fabulous. I love him."

"Me too," Jimmy said. "I love him."

The daughter-in-law?

"How about J.K.?" Bobby asked.

"Isn't J.K. on another show?" I asked.

"It doesn't matter," Jimmy said. "I love her."

"I couldn't love her more," Bobby said.

"I love her too," I said.

The used-car salesman?

"D.C. would be perfect," Bobby said. "I love D.C. Ben loves him too, don't you, Ben?"

"I love him," I said. "Love him."

"Wonderful," Jimmy said. "I love him myself."

July 24, 1977

"Here's why I called, George," the caller said. I sat in a glassed-in studio in the lobby of an office building in downtown L.A. while passers-by paused on benches and watched. "My question is about the Rockefellers. Does Mr. Stein really not know about the way they run things, or what?"

Outside the glass, a pretty tall brunette wearing a heavy silver cross picked at her teeth. She crossed her legs and yawned. I was tired too. I had plugged my book in four similar radio studios that week, although this was the first with spectators.

"I don't believe the Rockefellers run everything," I said. "I know a lot of people believe that, but I don't."

Out on the benches a collection of dispirited-looking people sat heavily and stared at me. Their faces sagged, as if they had been doomed to wander in shopping arcades until the Second Coming. A woman in late middle age, with a huge stomach and lipstick smeared on her face, painted her nails.

"Well, Mr. Stein," the caller said, his voice dripping with contempt, "you mean you don't believe this is all part of a one-world communistic plan?"

"Bircher," the talk show host whispered. The fifth one that hour.

A young black couple sat down on the benches and started to make faces at me as if I were a zoo animal. They stopped and lit cigarettes and took out a *Spiderman* comic book.

"I just don't believe in conspiracies generally," I said. "Maybe I should, but I don't. I'll think about it some more, though."

A pale girl with red hair and freckles sat down as if taking the weight of the world off her shoulders. She looked in at me and smiled. I wondered if she would pick me up as I left the studio.

"Mr. Stein," the caller said, "I just want to tell you that when the curtain comes down, you're going to be standing alone."

July 25, 1977

Two Hollywood jokes making the rounds:

One. the Shah flies to L.A. on a 747 with his son.
The son says, "Wow, what a great plane."
The Shah asks, "Do you like it?"
The son says, "I love it."
The Shah snaps his fingers. "I'll buy it for you."
The next day, they wander around the Beverly Hills Hotel.
The son says, "Wow, what a great place."
The Shah asks, "Do you really like it?"
The son says, "It's fabulous."
The Shah snaps his fingers. "I'll buy it for you."
That afternoon, they go down to Disneyland.
The son says, "Wow, what a great place."
The Shah asks, "Do you like it?"
The son says, "I love it."
The Shah starts to speak and the son says, "No, Dad. Don't buy me Disneyland. At the most, buy me a Mickey Mouse outfit."
So the Shah bought him NBC.
The second time I heard it, it was the William Morris Agency. The next time it was Columbia Pictures.

Two. Have you heard that a Polish conglomerate bought Paramount? Yes, and they're going to keep the same management. The second time I heard that, it also was Columbia Pictures.

July 26, 1977

The comedy variety show I have been working on is finished taping for a few months. I went to the "wrap party" last night at the Bistro restaurant, a fine and fancy place. A lot of my friends from the studio were there. My favorite, Tanya, offered me her cheek for a kiss, and then told me she was unhappy about something that she had seen in an article by me. "It would be good if you didn't write about that anymore," she said. "Is that all right? I don't want to have to sue you."

After an hour, the star of the show appeared with his girl friend. He is a funny guy who used to sing at small nightclubs and colleges. He played a role on *Mary Hartman* and then he was killed off. I begged our studio head not · to lose him, and he was saved for his own show, partly at my pleading request. When we first met, he called me "Ben" and was always full of jokes and pleasantries. When he got on the air, he started calling me "Benny," when he did not pass me without a word. Last night, after he had made it big, he saw me and said, "Well, look who's here." It's a standard line for people when they can't remember someone's name.

That ruined the party, even though the Bistro does make pretty good cannelloni.

July 28, 1977

Mike is dead. So is Rhonda. I found out this morning when I took out the dog. They were both found drowned at Ken Snyder's house in the hills, just off Sunset Boulevard. Ken Snyder came home to find them there. The newspaper showed a picture of Mike that must have been ten years old. He looked so young and enthusiastic that I could hardly remember him as he was. There was no picture of Rhonda.

The story said that Mike had just sold his interest in the record plant and the Riffmaster to Ken Snyder's company. Mike had a five-year $200,000-a-year contract with the company that bought him out.

I do not want to know how it happened. The article did not even mention Mike's wife. For all I know, she has left town. Whenever I asked Mike about her, he just said, "Forget that bitch."

And now she is probably reading the same article. I wonder if Mike knew what he was getting into. He probably knew that he was taking a chance. If he didn't, he was a fool.

But I wonder what I would do if Ken Snyder offered me a million dollars for my next book.

I liked Mike. Rhonda was a hopeless case, but Mike was full of energy and ambition. I saw a lot of myself in him. I hope he went quickly.

The funeral will be in Florida, where Mike's mother lives.

When I got back to my work after I read about Mike and Rhonda, I wondered why I even thought about the dildo factory or any of Mike's deals. There was something seductive about the easy money aspect of it all, something flashy about the notion of getting rich by "operating" instead of producing anything useful. I sat at the Palm and watched the people it had happened to and it made me want for it to happen to me, too.

But it was never me. Mike was right. I do like to sit in my little office and write. I love the sun and the girls and the palm trees. But most of all, I love the creation, the dreamlike way L.A. pulls thoughts from me and puts them down on the page, the way L.A. gets me to do things I always wanted to do.

The car is wonderful, and I sometimes feel that when I sit in it and glide along the Sunset Strip, everything that ever was is all there. But that is not right. Something is only all there if you can do it without money, without cars, without meals at the Palm. The rest is the icing, but the writing is what you live on and for.

That and the girl with the blue-green eyes. I hope Mike realized that sometime before he drowned.

July 29, 1977

The girl with blue-green eyes told me this morning that she has been writing again. It is something new. It's not the story of apocalypse she was once writing.

"It's nothing special," she said. "Maybe I shouldn't even be doing it."

I didn't say anything.

"I did want to get something done," she said.

"I think I figured out that your life is your art," I told her, and she started to cry. Tears of joy.

August 2, 1977

Lunch yesterday with my friend Lenny. We were going to go to the Palm, but he was in a hurry, so we went to Denny's, which is a family-type place, but not bad.

We sat at a semicircular booth of purple plastic, facing a woman in shorts and a floppy shirt with three children carrying banners from Disneyland.

"Which would you like with your lunch, sir?" the waitress asked. "Garlic bread or biscuits?"

"I'd better have biscuits," I said. "I have an appointment with Larry Goldberg after lunch."

Lenny leaned forward conspiratorially. "Do you think a Goldberg will *not* have garlic on his breath?" he asked.

I did not quite get it, since Lenny is Jewish and so am I. It was a joke, as it happened, and I was too sensitive. But I still don't get it.

"Here's the plan," Lenny said. "We're going to make a ten-part series about life in the twenties. You understand?" I understood. "It'll be a romance. A real sob story. We want to make a book deal at the same time." I waited expectantly. "Are you interested?"

Of course, I am always interested in that kind of thing. Who wouldn't be? But I keep getting my heart broken, and I am not interested in that. Still, I told him I was dying to do it. He asked me how I would put together the deal, and that worried me then and there. He was supposed to be the expert on that.

Sometimes I wonder if the whole thing is the same as being offered vacation land in Arizona. Still, I am interested, and I will pursue it. No one wants to be poor. Not in L.A.

August 15, 1977

A true Hollywood story: Last year I wrote a book, a novel. After some aggravation, I sold an option on the book for much less than I wanted. "Take less," the agent said. "It'll help you get other deals."
So I took less.
A few months ago, the folks who had bought the option asked me if I minded if the book was made into a TV movie instead of a theatrical movie. "It'll mean less money," the option holder said, "but it'll help you get other deals."
So I agreed to it.
This afternoon, a representative of a huge studio told me that his studio was interested. "It'll have to be for a lot less than what we've been talking about," he said, "but I'd take it if I were you, because that's going to help you get a lot of deals."
I hesitated. "Really," he said, "the first one is the hardest. After that, they're easy. Take a little less this time." His voice had a confiding, brotherly tone, I think, although I don't have a brother.
The human stock market again, trying to get me down to the lowest possible price. But I am a human being and not a stock, and this hurts. More writing, less hustling. That is what it all says.

August 17, 1977

Yesterday, I drove up to Arvin, California, with the girl with the blue-green eyes. Arvin is in the San Joaquin Valley, just east of Bakersfield, in a flat plain that opens suddenly after you reach the Tejon pass in the Tehachapis. The San Joaquin Valley, only an hour and a half from L.A., could not be farther removed from the world of flash, cash and trash. Arvin, a small farming community, is populated almost exclusively by former Okies who came to California during the Great Depression. None of them got rich, but they made a living and grew to be proud of who they were and what they had endured. The town lies at the end of a row of palm trees in a wide space on Kern County Highway 233.

Most of the buildings in Arvin are low cement structures with flat fronts, painted signs and one large picture window. The stores and repair shops and the one café are all painted various pastels—pink, blue, brown, orange, yellow. On the sidewalk of the one block of downtown is a list of the churches of Arvin. Southern Baptist, Church of the Nazarene, Pentecostal, Full Gospel, Tabernacle, and the other faiths that were carried in those tin lizzies and Chevies across Route 66, with the dust bowl howling at the back of the mind, and visions of heaven ahead.

I went up there to see what it was like in a town full of old Okies. What did they think about now that a new drought was upon us? What do they think of doctors and lawyers buying all the land as a tax shelter? What do they think? I thought they deserved to have something written about them.

On our way back, across unending fields of cotton, we turned on the radio for the CBS news. At 3 P.M., the announcer came on and played a snatch of "Hound Dog" and I knew, before she said a word, that Elvis Presley was dead. I wondered how the people of Arvin would take it. They probably had a better understanding of him than I ever could. He was more one of them than one of me.

Driving across the eight-lane highway that leads into L.A., through the mountains that were getting covered with fog, I thought about Elvis a lot. I could remember him from elementary school, clear as a bell, singing "Blue Suede Shoes." I could remember him singing "Loving You" in eighth grade, while I danced close with girls for the first time. I could remember him singing "Too Much" and the hard guys and hard girls at the one movie theater in my suburb grooving along with it while I stared out at them from behind the books I carried under my arm.

There was his sneer, and there his pompadour, and there his baby fat, and there his pink Cadillac, and there his army uniform, and there his bride and his baby, and there his mansion, and there him in a white jumpsuit at the Las Vegas Hilton. I remembered the crowd in Vegas, screaming when they saw him, screaming with the longing of a lifetime to be part of a man who was salvation in sequins and satin scarves.

And tucked away in my cartons as I moved around the country and back and forth from California were his records, incredibly old-fashioned-looking 45's, with pictures of him in his farm-boy outfit from *Love Me Tender.*

And suddenly he was dead at forty-two. People told me that Elvis was blowing five grams of coke a day in the last year. I do not know at all. I don't even care that much, except that it probably killed him. He was dead, and all the things I associated with him went floating around and out the funnel of time so that I felt as if twenty-one years had passed by in an instant of the CBS news.

I was lucky I heard about it on the way back from Arvin, because if I had heard it on Sunset Boulevard, it might not have made me think so much. But driving back from Arvin, while semis and diesels passed me, I had time to think.

And I thought about an eighteen-year-old Elvis, driving a truck, who becomes a star in a few days, and has more money and more money and more money, and women, and houses, and cars, and then drugs, and then dies one day, fully clothed, on his bedroom floor, at the age of forty-two. What if someone had told him that death at forty-two on a bedroom floor was what lay ahead? What would he have done? Would he have kept on driving that truck?

I want to know the answer because it tells me something about every kind of wanting to be a star, and a lot of people I know want to be stars and so do I. What was Elvis telling us?

Last night I bought an Elvis album with his wonderful "I Was the One." I have wanted that song and that album for twenty years and I got it last night and played that song twenty times, sitting in my living room watching the rain fall on the valley.

This afternoon, as I drove home from the studio, KRTH played Elvis's record of "Old Shep." It's about a boy whose old dog, Shep, is going blind. The vet tells him that the dog is dying and the vet cannot do any more. The boy tries to shoot the dog to put him out of his pain. He wants to kill himself instead. I cried for about two hours when I heard that song.

Later, a friend called me. He's in the record business. Someone had called him from North Carolina and said that he was crippled and losing his sight. He has a daughter who is losing her sight too. He loves Elvis. His daughter loves Elvis too. They have every one of his albums. The caller wanted to know how much he could get for them. I think the people in Arvin could tell him how much those records are worth.

August 18, 1977

Life on the fault line: Last night I stopped at a gas station on Laurel Canyon Road in the Valley. The gas station attendant, an Iranian, told me that my car was just what he wanted. "To me," he said, "it is beautiful."

I thanked him for the compliment and paid him. He gestured sourly at the surrounding sprawl of Sears and other low-rise shopping meccas.

"Why do you bring a car like this one here?" he asked disapprovingly. I do not know. The car has its life and I have mine.

This morning as I drove down to pick up Sarah, my maid, I pulled up next to a gleaming blue Cadillac convertible. As usual in Hollywood with Cadillac convertibles, there were two neatly groomed homosexuals at the helm. Their short hair, neatly trimmed mustaches and emaciated physiques wrapped in tight T-shirts marked them as part of L.A.'s thriving gay culture. Both men were playing tambourines. As I pulled up next to them, the driver shouted at me, "Hey, beautiful car."

Sometimes I think that my car has somehow eclipsed me. I am back somewhere I was a long time ago, and my car has gone on ahead.

Lunch today at a vegetarian restaurant on the Strip. Thin, weaselly-looking men with beards and slight stoops, peering forward, pulling out the wrinkles in their thin leather jackets, sit with skinny, angry-looking girls with coiffed hair and thick lips, in frilly sundresses or jeans and T-shirts. They stab at the cream cheese and date-nut bread and salads as if at the end of the meal either the eater or the eaten would be left.

A few feet away, on the Strip, eight lanes of traffic roar

by. The sun is blindingly bright and dazzling. It washes out all the colors of the restaurant, of the topless place across the street, of the streetwalkers who pass by, wrapped tightly, lips heavily painted, tottering on platform shoes.

I sat there and ate vegetable soup. Out of the dusty parking lot came a beautiful girl with pale, lovely skin, an erect carriage, a lacy sand-colored dress and a wide-brimmed floppy hat. She surveyed the scene of the restaurant and sat down at a table near me. I glanced at her but she looked away.

Apparently she decided that she was better off reading. From her straw pocketbook she took a magazine. I squinted into the sun to see what it was. L.A. is ever surprising. It was *The American Scholar*. Even if it was a prop, it was a good prop.

August 19, 1977

This afternoon, the girl with blue-green eyes came over with an outline and a first chapter of a book.

"It's just junk," she said. "Maybe you shouldn't read it."

I knew she wanted me to read it, and I did.

It was about a family from the Midwest with a strong streak of romanticism which persists down through three generations. The first chapter was wonderful.

"You can sell this in thirty minutes," I said.

"I don't know if I want to," she said, looking coy. "It's the story of my family."

"Will anyone else write it?" I asked.

She understood right away. "What agent should we go to?" she asked.

"We'll think about it," I said. "We'll take our time."

For the first time since I had seen her at the all-night Mayfair on Santa Monica, she looked as if she had time. Something about her doing that chapter gave her relief from obsessions about souls and "real people."

From my bedroom, without getting out of bed, you can see the lights for thirty miles out into the Valley. I watched them for a long time after the girl with blue-green eyes had fallen asleep. After a long time, but well before dawn, most of them go off.

August 20, 1977

A meeting this morning with a powerful honcho at ABC. The offices of ABC are in a giant granite office block in Century City, which sits low and squat on haunches of stone and steel, as if waiting to pounce upon an unsuspecting world. I wandered for a half hour in an underground parking maze more difficult by many orders of magnitude than anything I had encountered before. It was vast and deserted in the middle of a business day. My car echoed as its tires squealed around cement pillars. At any moment the Minotaur might appear.

Upstairs, at ABC, I walked into a reception room of Pharaonic dimensions. Two, not one, but two secretaries sat behind a massive wood-and-stone desk. Next to them were columns of steel and wood holding up the skylight ceiling three stories above. Glaring sunlight poured in through a three-story-high window behind the secretaries. Mammoth couches, as if made for a nervous serpent, lined the walls. It all reminded me of Albert Speer's design for a similar entrance for the Reich Chancery. It would be designed, the Führer said, to cow and frighten all those who passed through.

In fact, the ABC honcho was down-to-earth and cheerful. He listened attentively and made notes on a sheet of lined yellow paper. He giggled and laughed at the right places, and then smiled some more.

When the meeting broke up, my colleagues from the production company drifted down the hall. The man from ABC took my arm and asked me, "Do you have a deal with those guys?"

"Not yet," I said.

"Let's talk someday soon," he said with a wink.

At the elevator, my colleagues were grinning. "How much did he offer you?" one asked.

The other one shook his head. He pointed his chin at me. "This guy's a fucking hustler," he said.

I didn't mind. I know what I am, and it's not a hustler. I know that now after what happened to Mike. He was right. I am a writer, and not a hustler. I had no trouble finding my way out of the garage.

August 21, 1977

A big day yesterday. I think it marks the end of at least a large phase of my Hollywood living.

For the entire time I have been here, I have been searching for the perfect Hollywood home. When I lived in New York, I read the real estate section of *Daily Variety*, trying to imagine what the houses looked like and which I would have. In my mind, I saw myself in a white adobe Spanish house with French doors opening onto a breezy poolside lanai. I saw myself sitting in a darkened living room, thinking brilliant thoughts while below me the lights of the city stretched off for forty miles.

The reality was different. Most of the houses I could afford were 1950s-style monstrosities with plywood doors, wallboard, no view, no pool, and a smell of cats. The house I bought last winter was a fine house, but it was small and it had no pool. So I kept looking.

I looked at Spanish-style houses all over the city. Some were too big and some too small. They hardly ever struck that magic note. Yesterday I bought one that did. It sits high above the city. French doors open onto a breezy poolside lanai. There is a guesthouse and a greenhouse. It is just right for me. The only question is whether I can afford it. But if I can, and I think I can, then something miraculous will have happened.

By my own exertions, I will have got the house of my dreams, the kind of house I would want to live in if I were told that I had only a year to live, God forbid.

Sometimes I think of when I lived in Brooklyn Heights, a dark and cheerless part of New York, graced only by a wonderful view of lower Manhattan. Like a Dickensian character, I scurried along Pierrepont Street to my miserable apartment, locked inside against the dark and the chill and the rain.

Now I will lie in the sun and think creative thoughts. And this is what L.A. is about.

And L.A. is also about Danny. Danny left the cocaine trade a few months ago and started to write. He had saved money, so he did not work, or want to. He stayed inside all day and night, sending out for his groceries. When I saw him, he looked like a drowned rat. His hair was dirty and matted. His eyes were bloodshot. His clothes were wrinkled and smelled. His apartment began to look like it belonged to a junkie. Which it did.

Danny once made hilarious jokes. In the last few weeks, he makes more jokes than ever before, but they hardly ever hit the mark. He is no longer all there. He has a cold all the time and his nose has started to bleed. He talks mostly about the friends who have made it and wonders why he has not.

Yesterday I went out to visit him at the beach. He is living in a house at the Malibu Beach Colony which has been temporarily abandoned by its owner. When I got there, Danny was nowhere in sight. I pushed open the door. The house was empty. On the floor were ugly dark smudges. I called out and a drugged voice answered me. Danny was curled up on a mattress in a filthy little room. And that, I thought, was the story of Danny. In the Beach Colony, the fanciest spot in Southern California, Danny lay on a soiled mattress in a bare room. Danny was too stoned to talk, so I left.

That night I went to a party given by two of the most talented writers in America. They have a house on the beach. In their tiled living room we sat, the beautiful people and I. There was an English lord, several people whom I had seen at Leon's, a tall novelist of disaster themes, a fabulously rich inventor turned producer, and several actors and actresses. We all talked about England, school busing, record promotion, bookselling and the like. People listened when I spoke. I listened when they spoke.

A producer told a story about how his heart stopped beating after a routine operation. He was in the recovery room, still under anesthesia, when he felt himself leaving his body and watching his body lying there, his heart stopped. He felt blissfully calm and serene. Still under deep anesthesia, his voice cried out, "I think I'm going to faint" as a nurse passed by. The nurse took his pulse, found none, and began extraordinary measures. He was saved.

"I felt so good about that," he said, "that the whole thing has given me a much better feeling about life. And also about death."

I drove home alone along the Pacific Coast Highway. On my right I could hear the surf crashing against the sand. Above me were clear, balmy skies and bright stars. I felt wonderful, listening to the radio, hearing my car purring powerfully along the empty highway. The producer's story made me think of L.A. Something in me told me, years ago, that I must leave Washington, and then that I must leave New York, and come to L.A. I did it, and I was saved. I awoke from a thirty-year coma and became alive under the palm trees.

I often feel a swell of love for Los Angeles, driving along Hollywood Boulevard or Fountain Street or Beverly Drive or anywhere. There is something about the city that makes me feel euphoric. I cannot explain it. It has something to do with the climate and the sunlight and the freeways and the free people.

"But those people are so sad," the girl with blue-green eyes says. "They are so pitiful."

She is talking about Roxanne and Rhonda and R. and Mike and Lisa and maybe others too. "I don't think they're that sad," I tell her. "They're doing things. They get out in the sun. They can see the same palm trees. They can go to the beach or to the desert. They aren't living where they never see the sun shine."

But even that is not why L.A. is so wonderful. It has something to do with freedom, the ability to become what you want to become. Everything is mobile, moving, un-fixed here. Roxanne and Rhonda and even Mike could dream bold dreams and see them come true, no matter how briefly. The dreams of Roxanne and Rhonda are not the same as the dreams of David Rockefeller or Kingman Brewster, but they are real dreams no less.

And then there are my dreams. The car and the girls and the Spanish house are only the outward appearances of the dreams that have come true in L.A. For me, L.A. means doing and being free. And that is why I love it.

"It's just the place for you," the girl with blue-green eyes says. "You can't explain it all," she says, and she is right. I am not going to try any longer.

As I thought that, I could see the lights of Santa Monica twenty miles down the coast. I stepped down on the accel-erator and opened the sun roof. The night air and the sound of waves on the beach swept through the car. I headed for L.A. My car roared forward and I was in it.